Liu Bin's
Zhuang Gong
Bagua Zhang

勤婢橘场八卦

Liu Bin's Zhuang Gong Bagua Zhang

SOUTH DISTRICT BEIJING'S STRONGLY ROOTED STYLE

Foundation Practices, Volume One

Zhang Jie WITH Richard Shapiro

BLUE SNAKE BOOKS
BERKELEY, CALIFORNIA

Published by Blue Snake Books
Blue Snake Books' publications are distributed by
North Atlantic Books
P.O. Box 12327
Berkeley, California 94712

Cover photo: Initiation ceremony for the students of Master Liu Bin, 1920. Photo courtesy Zhang Jie; photographer unknown.

Cover and book design by Jan Camp.

Printed in the United States of America.

Liu Bin's Zhuang Gong Bagua Zhang is sponsored by the Society for the Study of Native Arts and Sciences, a nonprofit educational corporation whose goals are to develop an educational and cross-cultural perspective linking various scientific, social and artistic fields; to nurture a holistic view of the arts, sciences, humanities and healing; and to publish and distribute literature on the relationship of mind, body, and nature.

PLEASE NOTE: The creators and publishers of this book disclaim any liabilities for loss in connection with following any of the practices, exercises, and advice contained herein. To reduce the chance of injury or any other harm, the reader should consult a professional before undertaking this or any other martial arts, movement, meditative arts, health, or exercise program. The instructions and advice printed in this book are not in any way intended as a substitute for medical, mental, or emotional counseling with a licensed physician or healthcare provider.

North Atlantic Books' publications are available through most bookstores. For further information, call 800-733-3000 or visit our website at www. northatlanticbooks.com. or www.bluesnakebooks.com.

Library of Congress Cataloguing-in-Publication Data

Zhang, Jie, 1945–
Liu bin's zhuang gong bagua zhang: foundation practices, volume one / by Zhang Jie with Richard Shapiro.
     p. cm.
ISBN 978-1-58394-218-5
1. Hand-to-hand fighting, Oriental. I. Shapiro, Richard, 1969– II. Title.
GV1112.Z425 2008
796.815—dc22
                                                                                2007052361

1 2 3 4 5 6 7 8 9 SHERIDAN 14 13 12 11 10 09 08

ACKNOWLEDGMENTS

I would like to thank all my students and friends across the U.S. and in China. Since I started working on this book, I have been back to China three times to visit with and talk to Masters Ti En Fang, Teng Hao Lin, Xu Sheng Li, Yang Yong Li, Bai Yu Tsai, Wang Zheng Ting, Li Zong Chuan, Han De, and others. These masters were able to give me very important pieces of information about Bagua Zhang. Master Ti En Fang talked to me about the secrets of Bagua Zhang and Chinese culture that he has studied for nearly seventy years. Master Xu Sheng Li gave me some special pictures and talked to me about the secret of single palm change with the Bai Ko Huan Bu. Master Xu Sheng Li also came with me when I went to talk with all of the old masters of South District Bagua Zhang; because Master Xu is very well respected and trusted, these masters were very open with their knowledge when he accompanied me. Master Teng Hao Lin talked to me about the history of South District Bagua Zhang. (Master Teng used to study with Liu Shi Kui, beginning in 1935, and his father and grandfather were both masters of South District Bagua Zhang—he knew the history of it very well.) Masters Bai Yu Tsai and Wang Zheng Ting gave me information about Master Wang Wen Kui. Han De introduced me to Master Teng Hao Lin, and also gave me a lot of information about his grandfather, Master Han Wu. Master Li Zong Chuan introduced me to the leaders of the martial arts association of Beijing and the Bagua Zhang association of Beijing. All of these people have supported me to finish this book, and I am grateful to everyone for all the help I have received.

I especially want to thank my student and friend Richard Shapiro. He and his wife Alyson started studying Bagua with me in 2000. When Richard learned about my plans to write this book, and that I was worried that my English was not good enough, he offered to help me without pay. We both believed we had a great chance to research and study the art of

Bagua Zhang and Chinese culture more deeply and more systematically than ever before. Since we started, we've worked together almost every week and his help has been invaluable. There has always been a great harmony between us.

There were many ways in which Richard's background helped in writing this book. He has a master's degree in exercise and sports science, he has a clear understanding of Bagua Zhang, and he always knows the English words for what I am talking about. Richard didn't just type what I talked about. He had good questions for me, which gave me a chance to think deeply about Bagua Zhang and to discover new and useful things about it. Richard has helped me uncover deeper truths about Bagua Zhang and to explain it in the best way possible. In addition, Richard spent a lot of time photographing my Bagua Zhang movements, a very important part of this book. His photos will help people understand, study, and practice Bagua Zhang much more easily. I am also very thankful to Alyson, who understood and supported Richard's work with me.

Richard and I plan to write more books on the Bagua Zhang system, as well as the Guo Lin Chi Gong cancer therapy system. I believe these kinds of books can help people to understand Chinese culture, the world, and themselves, and to achieve greater harmony in life. We need harmony and peace in the world.

A NOTE FROM RICHARD SHAPIRO

As Zhang Jie and I were working on this book, I was constantly amazed at how rich and developed Bagua Zhang is. There is so much important information, so many stories, and so many forms. My wife Alyson would often say, "You have enough for two or three books already. When are you going to stop?"

Alyson was right: when we brought our manuscript to Blue Snake Books, they wanted to make it much shorter. This book is only about half of the material we had already worked on. Our next book will contain the other half: the history of the other South District Bagua masters, more advanced Bagua theory, the Eight Fists/Palms/Elbows Form, the Five Elements/Twenty-Four Movements Form, the Eight Mother Palms Form, the Heaven Sword Form, and the Earth Staff Form. In future books, Professor Zhang intends to look at more advanced forms, weapons forms, two-person drills, and more. But this first book gives you a good basis to begin to understand the essence of Bagua Zhang.

When reading this book, you will notice that there are often several names for what is essentially the same thing. For example, Zhuang Gong Bagua, Cheng Bagua, Cheng Pai Liu Shi Bagua, Liu Bin's Bagua, Beijing South District Bagua, and more are all names for the style of Bagua Zhang talked about in this book. This is a very common practice in Chinese arts and culture: each name describes or shows a side of the thing, but words cannot fully express the essence of the thing. If you can understand this point and get used to thinking this way, it will be much easier to understand the way of Chinese thinking, Chinese culture, and of course, Bagua Zhang.

TABLE OF CONTENTS

INTRODUCTION

Bagua Zhang is one of the Chinese internal martial arts, which also include Taiji Chuan and Hsing-I Chuan, but it is also more than simply a martial art. Bagua has a very special and deep relationship with traditional Chinese culture, and has absorbed many of its parts—philosophy, medicine, chi gong, morality, and art. It is rare for one art to have absorbed so many different elements, and this makes Bagua a special gem of Chinese culture. Through a deep and thorough study and practice of the art of Bagua, you can understand every part of Chinese culture.

Master Dong Hai Chuan was the first person to show and teach the art of Bagua Zhang to the public, but the history and development of Bagua Zhang go back much further than his teachings. Bagua grew within the Chinese culture much in the way that a baby grows in its mother. When a baby is in its mother's body, you cannot see it as it develops. Once the baby is born, you can see it all at once, but in truth it has been a long time in the making.

The practice of Bagua Zhang can assist you in understanding Chinese culture and thought in a direct, experiential way. By this, I mean to say that Bagua Zhang is like a big book. You use your eyes, your mind, and your body to "read the book" as you practice. It takes time, but it will bring you to the great hall of Chinese culture, and teach you how to appreciate and understand it. All cultures, whether Greek, Indian, Chinese, or Western, whether modern or traditional, have at their core a philosophy, a way of doing things. The goal of any culture is to promote harmony among its people and between people and nature. And in all of these cultures, the highest level of human development is morality. Bagua Zhang is very much a product of the Chinese way of thinking and doing things, but at its center are the universal goals of harmony and morality. This makes Bagua much more than a fighting system. Yes, there are techniques that can be used for self-defense or fighting, but the practice of Bagua Zhang also teaches the student how to create harmony out of disorder. The essence of Bagua Zhang is philosophy, morality, health, peace, and harmony. This is why I call Bagua Zhang a merciful martial art.

In the beginning of the nineteenth century Master Dong Hai Chuan brought Bagua Zhang to Beijing from Jiu Hua Mountain, and it quickly became a very famous martial art. Master Dong taught a lot of students, and many of them became great masters and developed their own schools of Bagua Zhang: Yin Fu Bagua, Cheng Ting Hua Bagua, Song Chang Rong Bagua, and others. The Bagua I am talk about in this book is the Bagua of Liu Bin. Master Liu Bin was one of the best students of Master Cheng Ting Hua, who in turn was one of the best students of Master Dong.

All of the masters' work in developing this martial art has brought Bagua Zhang to a very high level of development. Their work has made it possible for people of the modern world to practice Bagua Zhang. This is one of the principle things that culture can do—it can help people develop the arts and sciences, to make them more useful, more elegant, and more understandable. The living culture of China has helped to make this martial art flourish and grow. But each generation had to do its part. They had a strong responsibility to keep the culture—its arts, crafts, and philosophies—alive, growing, and changing, without losing the essentials.

In different times there are different responsibilities, questions, environments, and people. The Bagua of different times reflects those differences. But the essence of Bagua, the principles, remains the same; the form changes, but not the essentials. This is important for English-speaking people who practice Bagua to understand, because they have a very different culture from that of China a hundred years ago. But the essence of human beings practicing Bagua Zhang doesn't change from one side of the ocean to the next, or from year to year.

I've taught Bagua to many students, and before they started practicing they told me they often felt tired and stressed. But after practicing Bagua, the stress and tiredness were gone, replaced by good energy and balanced emotions. This is because Bagua practice opens your whole body to the universe. The circulation of chi and blood gets developed, and negative energy, such as tension, stress, and negative emotions, is removed through the body's channels and points. Good chi enters your body and becomes positive internal chi that supports your life.

It is up to each person to be a good Bagua student. You have to strive to understand, to practice, and to develop your art within yourself. If you can do this, you will be learning more than just Bagua—you will be learning how to live life well.

Why I Decided to Write This Book

Since coming to this country from China in 1990, I have taught Bagua, Taiji Chuan, and chi gong, as well as Chinese medicine, philosophy, calligraphy, and culture. People have always asked me to write about these subjects, but I haven't done so until now because I was still looking to find the best way to talk to people about Chinese culture. For example, most people who practice Bagua hold the opinion that Bagua is one of the best martial arts in China. That is correct, but that isn't enough—Bagua is also very close to the essence of Chinese culture itself. If you can imagine Chinese culture as a huge fruit tree, Bagua could be looked upon as one of the fruits that has come from the tree. But the fruit also contains the seeds of that tree inside itself. Or if you picture the whole system of Chinese culture as a big building, Bagua can be seen as a special door to lead you inside. And after you get into the building and look back at the Bagua, you can see much more clearly what it is.

I think that I also needed to continue my own studying and research of both Bagua and Chinese culture. Both of them were like a big mountain in front of my face—I needed to look up at them with a feeling of respect. When you consider that Chinese culture is over 5,000 years old, I am a very young student. I needed to wait. But now I can tell that the time has come; this is the right moment for me to write a book about Bagua.

For me, writing this book has felt like walking through the great hall of the Bagua Zhang martial arts system, and through the big golden mountain of Chinese culture. Over the course of making the book, we never felt tired, but were always happy and excited. All of the treasures of Chinese culture and Bagua Zhang come to my mind like pictures from a movie, everything I have studied over the last fifty years of my life: Chinese philosophy, morality, Confucius, Lao Tzu, poetry, literature, history, medicine, calligraphy, and especially Bagua Zhang. I can remember that first day when I began to practice Bagua Zhang in Tian Tan Park with my teacher, Liu Xing Han. I remember the times when my Bagua brothers and I were working on the first book of teacher Liu's Bagua Zhang. We were all working together very hard, no matter how cold in the winter, how hot in the summer. I remember Master Liu Xing Han's wife—we would call her "Shi Niang" (mother/teacher)—always making a wonderful meal for us while we were working in our teacher's home. I remember visiting my Bagua uncle Wang Wen Kui, when he would teach me many of the secrets of Bagua Zhang. I remember Master Li Zong Chuan working very hard to organize us for Master Liu's class and for the book, like a great general. I envisioned all of these people standing in front of my face, asking me to finish this book in English. I knew I was facing a big challenge, but I enjoyed it. This is the special job I was given from the masters of Bagua Zhang.

I am now sixty years old, a very important age. I have much more experience with life, Chinese culture, Bagua, and human beings. This book is like the beautiful fruit that comes in autumn—everything comes naturally in its own time. As I look back on my life, I have never stopped studying and thinking about Chinese culture. My experiences of difficult times in China, including famine and the Cultural Revolution, have made me want to share the treasure of Chinese culture with everyone—because we don't need famine, we don't need war, we don't need the whole world to be out of balance, we don't need problems between different countries and cultures. We need peace and a better life for everyone.

My Early Life and the Buddhist Monk

When I was three and a half years old in the summer of 1949, I had a very bad infection known as Kan Tou Chuang. People would often die from this. The regular doctor couldn't help me, so my mother took me to Da

Cheng, the big temple close to my home. People had told my mom there was a great Buddhist monk living there who could fix my health problems. Even though this happened fifty-nine years ago, I can still remember it very clearly. It was very hot, and we traveled to the temple in a rickshaw. When we arrived, the Buddhist monk was waiting at the door for us. My mother told him what the problem was: my neck was very swollen, and my throat was infected and painful. I also had a fever. He said, "Don't worry, I can help." He led us into the great hall of the temple and let me sit down on an old hardwood chair, facing south. My mother sat down on the other chair, facing west. The monk stood facing me, about twenty feet away.

Then he started prrying. He closed his eyes and began to chant softly. Then, one hand at a time, he made a grabbing movement to one side, then the other, as if gathering air. Then he took both hands and opened them toward me. I felt a very cold, soft wind come into my throat and neck. I stopped sweating, and I felt very comfortable and soothed. Then he did it two more times. After half an hour, I fell asleep. When I awoke, the pain was gone, the fever was gone, and the swelling was gone. Everything was fine. My mother asked, "Are you sure you are finished?" The monk told her he was. "How much do I owe you?" she asked. "Nothing," he replied.

At that time, I didn't understand what had happened. Now I know that it was a traditional Chinese chi gong treatment. The Buddhist monk was a great chi master and chi doctor. He may have saved my life.

Soon after the monk healed me with his chi treatment, when I was four years old, I was plrying in the street outside of my house one day. A big white horse came running south down the street, very fast and out of control. Somebody came out to try to stop the horse and it changed direction, running straight toward me. All my neighbors thought, "Oh no, that kid is dead!" But instead the horse kicked the wall right behind me and jumped over me. Again, my life was saved.

I believe that the Buddhist monk planted the special seed of Chinese culture in my life when he fixed my problem, a seed that gave me special energy and opened my mind and spirit. I believe that is why my life was saved again. I also believe it is why I became so interested in traditional

Chinese culture—including medicine, martial arts, and calligraphy—when I was a young boy. It is why I met a special teacher of Shaolin martial arts, Master Liu Xing Han, at a young age, and had the opportunity to study Bagua Zhang from him. It is also why I was able to survive the Cultural Revolution.

During the Cultural Revolution, the situation was so dangerous for students. Life was very hard during my time teaching in the countryside. There was not enough food and we were always hungry. There was no freedom to think or talk, and no books to read or study, except the "little red book." If you were intelligent and learned, if you looked around with your eyes open and thought with your own mind, you could be killed, put in prison, or "reeducated." But I couldn't change to conform; if I changed, I would have become a different person, not me. My life in China during this time was like a small boat moving on the big ocean of political life. Many times I felt the big waves would smash me and drown me, but somehow I always got away safe.

In 2001 I went back to Beijing to visit my family. I wanted to find the temple where the monk fixed my health problem, but I could not. Since 1950, Beijing has changed so much and many old buildings have been destroyed. The temple may be gone, but the spirit of that holy place is still in my heart forever.

Learning Shaolin

In the first year that I studied in a public school, at the age of seven, one of my best friends asked me if I wanted to learn martial arts. I said that I did. He said, "I know a great martial arts master. If you want to learn, I can introduce you to him." I asked who this master was, and my friend said, "He is my parents' neighbor. His name is Chang."

I really wanted to learn martial arts, so I asked my friend to introduce me to him. We went to teacher Chang's home. He lived nearby and was about thirty years old at the time. He was a master of Shaolin Gong Fu, but he didn't want people to know that he knew martial arts. He asked me about my parents and told me that he knew them. "Do you really want to study martial arts from me?" he asked. I said that I did. He said, "OK, come here with your friend tomorrow." My friend immediately kneeled down and formally asked him to be his teacher. I followed him, and the teacher said that my friend was now my "older brother" in gong fu.

I studied with teacher Chang for about two years, and then he stopped teaching because of the political situation in China; he was afraid of being known as a martial arts teacher. In 1966, right at the beginning of the Cultural Revolution, I met him on the street. He had had a stroke and was having a hard time walking. Very soon after, he passed away. He was my first martial arts teacher, and he was a great master of Shaolin. I remember how his movements were so fast and beautiful.

After getting a foundation of training with teacher Chang, I started opening my eyes and mind to traditional Chinese martial arts. I didn't find the martial arts; they came to me. It was a great gift from life. I believe that it happened because of my early experience with the Buddhist monk.

A Special Time and Place: Tian Chao and the South District of Beijing

My father moved to Beijing from his hometown of Renshu in Hebei province when he was twelve years old, in 1901. Over time he became an excellent tailor, and my parents lived in the south district of Beijing. Since the Ching dynasty in the sixteenth century, the south district of Beijing had become a center of popular culture, especially the Tian Chao ("Heavenly Bridge") area, which was the center of the south district of Beijing. There were many popular shows at Tian Chao, such as martial arts demonstrations, opera, movies, theatre, comedy shows, magic, public lectures, and wrestlers. The working class, government officials, and intellectuals alike would come to Tian Chao, and for a little money they could have a lot of fun and see many exciting things.

In the east of Tian Chao is Heaven Temple Park. The emperor and his government officials would go there in the springtime to pray for a good year. Inside Heaven Temple Park there are many old pine trees; some are over three or four hundred years old. Masters Dong Hai Chuan, Cheng

Ting Hua, Liu Bin, Wang Wen Kui, and Liu Xing Han all taught and practiced Bagua in this park. All of the old great masters of Bagua would go there to talk about Bagua, to practice, teach, and learn. Almost all of them also used to live around this area.

In Tian Chao many different martial arts schools mixed together, and everyone improved their skills by influencing each other. The great master of wrestling, Bao San, had his own area in Tian Chao where he and his students would practice, and people could pay to watch. The great martial arts master Chang Bao Zhong also had his own area to practice and demonstrate. He would practice with a huge sword that weighed over a hundred pounds and could draw six bows at once, using his hands, feet, and teeth!

My parents' home was very close to Tian Chao, and as I grew up I was lucky to be immersed in this center of culture and martial arts. Around 1950, when I was studying in primary school, my classmates and I would go to Tian Chao to watch and enjoy the wrestling, martial arts, and everything else. We would go almost every day after school. I really idolized Bao San and Chang Bao Zhong; for a young and energetic boy, they were heroes. During that time I was very close to traditional Chinese culture, and seeing them practice helped me to understand it even better.

At the same time, Masters Liu Shi Kui, Wang Wen Kui, and Li Yan Chin were practicing Bagua at Heaven Temple Park. At that time I didn't know about Bagua; I was just ten years old. I never saw them practicing there, but I now know they were there at that time. This whole environment had a strong influence on my life, and helped me develop a strong feeling for and understanding of Chinese culture.

In 1964 I graduated from high school and passed the national test—eighteenth in the whole country—that allowed me to attend Beijing University. I continued studying Chinese literature, philosophy, and history. Studying the culture of China in a broad way helped me to better understand the things I had come to love in the popular culture, which gave me a different understanding than most people.

The Cultural Revolution

During the Cultural Revolution, from 1966 to 1976, the Chinese people and culture had a very hard time. It was like an earthquake and a tsunami at the same time—there was much trouble for everyone, and great uncertainty as to how things would turn out.

In 1970, when I was a teacher in high school, I was among those the government sent to the countryside. I had a very hard time in the country because there wasn't enough food, there were no books for reading (except for Chairman Mao's book), and there was terrible stress because of the political situation. I felt like I was a prisoner, on the bottom of life. The Cultural Revolution kept me from being able to study Chinese culture, and this made me even hungrier to learn more when I could. Having it taken away helped me realize how valuable it was. In 1976, when the Cultural Revolution ended, China began to open its doors to the world. I passed the national test and moved back to Beijing to continue studying for my master's degree in Chinese culture, which I finished in 1978.

Liu Xing Han

In the springtime of 1979, I met my Bagua teacher, Master Liu Xing Han, in Heaven Temple Park.

Master Zhang Jie practices with his teacher, Master Liu Xing Han

Master Liu Xing Han was a fourth-generation master of Bagua Zhang, and the youngest student of Master Liu Bin. His father, Liu Zhen Zong, was a very close friend of Liu Bin; they were as close as brothers. When Liu Xing Han was a young boy, his father would practice together with Master Liu Bin and two other Bagua masters—Ji Feng Xiang and Wang Dan Lin—in their family home, almost every day. And so, Liu Xing Han grew up with Bagua Zhang. When the four older masters practiced or researched together, Liu Xing Han always watched them and paid attention to what was said and practiced. When he was a teenager, Liu Xing Han asked his father to teach him Bagua, but according to Chinese tradition a father never teaches his own son. So Liu Zhen Zong asked Liu Bin to teach his son Bagua instead. Liu Xing Han also continued to learn about Bagua from Masters Ji Feng Xiang and Wang Dan Lin, as well as from Liu Bin's son, Master Liu Shi Kui (the leader of the fourth generation of Bagua Zhang) and from Master Wang Wen Kui (who was one of the best students of Liu Bin).

Master Liu Xing Han kept practicing and researching Bagua Zhang throughout his whole life. He didn't stop even during the Cultural Revolution, but practiced in secret. Right after the Cultural Revolution, Master Liu Xing Han started to teach Bagua in Heaven Temple Park, where Masters Cheng Ting Hua and Liu Bin had taught. (Liu Xing Han had also taught Bagua before the Cultural Revolution, in the 1940s; his oldest student, Master Liu Jing Liang, moved to Yunan province, where he started to teach Bagua in 1950.) Master Liu Xing Han's students came from almost everywhere in the country. He was very well known as one of the best Bagua teachers of that time.

Passing on the Tradition of Bagua Zhang

Master Liu Xing Han was particularly interested in me as a Bagua student for two reasons. First, we were neighbors, and he and his wife knew my mother. Second, I had a special background in both martial arts and Chinese culture, which Master Liu considered a solid foundation for being a good Bagua student. My relationship with Master Liu Xing Han was like the old Chinese srying: "Two hands clapping together." You need both a good student and a good teacher to pass on the true Bagua. When I asked Master Liu if I could learn Bagua from him, he laughed and said, "I have the same question for you: do you want to learn Bagua from me?"

Master Zhang Jie practicing Jian, or sword, with Master Liu Xing Han

So I became an indoor student of Master Liu Xing Han in the spring of 1979, one of the most important times in my life. I studied with Master Liu at Heaven Temple Park almost every day. While training there, I met many Bagua masters: Wang Wen Kui, Wang Rong Tang, Wang Zhen Ting (Wang Wen Kui's son), Bai Yu Cai (Wang Wen Kui's best student), Han Wu (who studied with both Master Chang Guo Xing and Master Liu Shi Kui), He Pu Ren (a famous acupuncturist who studied under Master Yang Ming Shan), Li Zong Chuan (who was the president of Beijing Sports College and studied Bagua with Liu Xing Han), Zhu Zhen Hua (who studied with Liu Shi Kui), Li Wen Zhang (who was a great Bagua fighter and studied under Master Wang Rong Tang), and Han De (who is the grandson of Han Wu and the leader of the seventh generation of Cheng Bagua). We practiced together and did research work on Bagua theory and history.

Starting the Bagua Book

Beginning in 1976, China opened its doors to the world. People's lives were returning to normal, and they began practicing traditional Chinese culture once again. Almost every day, Masters Wang and Liu got letters from people who wanted to learn Bagua but who found it hard to find a teacher or even a good book on the subject. Masters Liu and Wang felt a responsibility to pass on the art of Bagua before it was lost.

In 1977, Master Liu said to Master Wang, "Brother, I think we need to write a book about Bagua. It is a treasure of Chinese culture, and many people will want to learn and understand it in the future." Master Wang Wen Kui agreed—between them, it was like two hands clapping, making a great sound.

The first task was to find others to help write the book. Master Liu Xing Han started a training group in Tian Tan Park (Heaven Temple Park) with the goal of finding and nurturing the most talented students. Very soon, people came to the training group from all over China. The group included Xie Fu De, from Shandong province; Xing Yun Cai, from Guangxi province; You De Gen, from Hunan province; Li Guo Gun, from Henan province; Xiao Hai Xue, from Guichou province; Liu Jing Liang (who was the oldest student of Liu Xing Han), from Yunan province; and many students from all over Beijing, including myself. All the students came from different backgrounds. The group included high school and college students, university professors, artists, sport coaches, and scientists. Master Liu Xing Han enjoyed teaching all of them. The main things he looked for in a student were good morals, a love of Bagua, and diligence in learning and practicing.

Every morning, Master Liu Xing Han would teach Bagua at Tian Tan Park for free. In the evening, he would continue to research and practice at his home. After three years, he started to choose people from the training group who would be able to help him with the book. He was the person chiefly responsible for the book, and he took his responsibilities very seriously. In addition to Master Wang Wen Kui, his advisor on the project, the writing group included Master Wang Rong Tang (a fourth-generation Bagua master who studied under Master Yang Ming Shan), Master Han Wu (a fifth-generation Bagua master who studied under Masters Zhang Guo Xiang and Liu Shi Kui), Ma Jian Xing (the president of the Beijing Sport Research Institute), Li Zong Chuan (the president of the Beijing Sports School and who studied under Liu Xing Han), Dr. He Pu Ren (the vice president of the Chinese Acupuncture Association and who studied under fourth-generation master Wang Dian Rong), Dr. He Xin, Dr. Zhao Min Hua, Master Wang Zhen Ting (the vice president of the Bejing Bagua Association and the son of Wang Wen Kui), Master Han De (the grandson of Han Wu), Master Cui Yu Ke (who studied under Liu Xing Han), Master Mei Hui Chi (who studied under Wang Rong Tang), Master Guo Xue Xin (who studied under Wang Rong Tang), Master Shing Mao Ting (who studied under Liu Xing Han), Master Liu Mao Shing (who studied under Liu Xing Han), Master Liu Chuang (the son of Liu Xing Han), and Ma Yu Kuan (a great painter). At the time I was a professor of Chinese culture at Beijing University, and I was also invited to be a part of the writing group. Everyone in this group loved Bagua, and the diversity of their backgrounds and experiences helped to make a good book.

From 1979 to 1982, we worked together every weekend on the book. Master Liu Xing Han and Master Wang Wen Kui organized and directed the writing and production of the book, and contributed old secrets that they had learned to put into the book as well. The two old masters had a good vision of the future. They understood that Bagua could be an important part of rebuilding Chinese culture and that writing a great book could benefit the whole world as well. They also both had big hearts—they were open to working with people from a variety of backgrounds. They were like two great generals in the army, leading us to victory. Like a light in the middle of the night, they helped guide us in the right direction. Together, they were like an encyclopedia of Bagua knowledge, and they always gave insightful answers to our questions.

In 1986 this book was published in Beijing—the first book written on Bagua since the start of the Cultural Revolution. It talked about the history of Bagua, the theory of the *I Ching,* the theory of medicine, and the most important foundation forms, including the palm forms and weapons forms. (Parts of the first book by Master Liu Xing Han's writing group can be found in several works on Bagua in English. But nobody who has translated this book has been involved with the people who wrote it in Chinese, and I am not sure that they understand it very well at all.) After the book was published, the other students went back to their own places

xxiv — Liu Bin's Zhuang Gong Bagua Zhang

to open new Bagua schools, planting the seeds of Bagua Zhang across the whole country.

The Growth and Renewal of Bagua Zhang

The first publication run was 19,600 copies, but the demand was so great that many people couldn't find a copy. Masters Liu and Wang got a lot of letters from people, not only from around China but from other countries, asking when the next book would come out. The readers told them how much they liked the book, how thankful they were for it, and how much the book had helped them understand Bagua and Chinese culture. Like a phoenix, Chinese culture and Bagua had risen from the "fire" to live and thrive in the world of today.

Master Liu told me an interesting story that happened after the book was published. He spent a month vacationing at his daughter's home in north Beijing. He saw a group of young men practicing Bagua in a nearby park and Master Liu stopped to watch them. He told them they were doing Bagua wrong and he demonstrated the form. They were very unhappy about this—he could tell from their expressions that they didn't think an old man knew much about Bagua. They said, "Who are you? How do you know about Bagua? Are you a Bagua master?"

"I know some Bagua," Master Liu said. Then he asked them, "Who is your teacher?"

"We don't have a teacher," they replied.

So Liu asked, "How did you learn Bagua without a teacher?"

The young men said, "This is our teacher!" and showed Master Liu a copy of his book. They said it was a great book.

"Do you know who wrote this book?" Master Liu asked them.

"No, we wish we could know him, but that will never happen!" they replied.

Master Liu just smiled. He had such a good feeling of balance and awareness that the young men began to get suspicious. So they asked him, "What is your name, sir?"

"I am Liu Xing Han!"

The young students were so surprised and happy. "Oh, you are the master!" they said. "Can we be your students?"

"Yes," Master Liu said, "I would like to teach all of you. But I live and teach in the south district of Beijing. If you get the chance, you are welcome to come to my class in Tian Tan Park." The young students were very happy, and after that some of them would ride their bicycles three or four hours each way to Tian Tan Park to learn Bagua from Master Liu.

After the book's publication, people flocked to Beijing from all around China to become students of Masters Liu and Wang. In August 1989, we had a big celebration and initiation ceremony for Master Liu's students. The initiation ceremony comes from traditional Chinese culture, and this one had several special meanings. In the ceremony, students show respect to their teachers, and through the respect shown to the teacher, they show their respect for and love of the Bagua martial arts system. This initiation ceremony was also important because it allowed new students to be recognized by the larger Bagua community. The ceremony also brought together the entire Bagua community in Beijing, so they could learn from one another. Finally, the ceremony showed the strength and endurance of the Bagua system as a part of Chinese culture, still alive and well in Beijing. The cover picture of this book was taken at the initiation ceremony for the students of Master Liu Bin, back in 1920.

Over time, if more people know and respect Bagua, then more young students will naturally want to learn Bagua. It is the best advertisement for promoting the art of Bagua.

More Books on Bagua

After the first book was published, Master Liu Xing Han, Master Li Zong Chuan, Master Han De, Master Li Hou Pei, and I started to work on a second book, which was published in 1993. At the same time, Master Liu Jing Liang, Master Li Zong Chuan, and I had finished another Bagua book with the assistance of Master Liu Xing Han, called *Bagua Zhang*. It was finished just before I left for the United States in 1990 and was published in 1992.

The second and third books continued to talk more about Bagua, and included the Sixty-Four Palms of Si Zheng Si Yu (Four Corners, Four Directions), Nine Palaces Walking, sword form, Double Zi Wu Yin Yang Yuan Yang Yue, spear form, Five Elements Bagua Kicks, Seven Stars Short Staff Form, and applications for many of these forms. The purpose of the second and third books was to teach students how to develop and advance their Bagua skills after they had thoroughly practiced the techniques in the first book, which was the most important.

Three Dreams in the United States

When I came to the United States in 1990 to lecture on traditional Chinese culture, I had a hard time at first. I didn't speak English well, and I missed China and my friends very much. I was living by myself in Seattle, and I was very depressed. One night I had a dream that I was walking out of a beautiful, classic Chinese building. I heard a voice from the heavens say, "I know that you want to see god. Please look up to the sky—god is there." I looked up to the sky, and I saw a very bright light. The light grew and made the whole sky bright. I thought, "Oh, is that god?"

I woke up and called a friend of mine. "What does this mean?" I asked her. I was not a religious man and had never had any of these kinds of experiences. My friend said, "I think you are right; that was god."

Almost a year later, my student Jonathan and I took a ferryboat to Orcas Island to see some of my patients and students there. Many tourists were there on the boat, talking loudly. I told Jonathan that I wanted to meditate and sat down on a big chair. Soon, my mind and my body became very relaxed and quiet, and I couldn't hear the noise from the tourists. All of a sudden I saw nothing but a beautiful blue color—my favorite color. I could feel that the circulation of my chi was very smooth, and I could feel the chi moving in circles around my Dan Tian, the energy center of the body. I had never had such a strong and comfortable feeling of the chi before.

Then I saw the Buddha sitting on the right side of me. His body was huge, like a mountain. His face was round like the moon, with a very beautiful smile, and he had very short, black, curly hair. He had on a long robe of yellow and red, and was sitting in a prayer position. I thought,

"Why would the Buddha come? I never think about him. Is this a dream?" I tried to move my vision, but the image of the Buddha followed me. Wherever I looked, he was showing me a smile and giving me a peaceful feeling. Then, the Buddha showed me a mudra, or symbolic hand posture. He closed his eyes and put his hand to the side of his face, telling me to sleep. I thought, "Oh, the Buddha wants me to take a rest." So I copied his movement and lay down for a while.

When I opened my eyes, everyone had left the boat. I had been deeply asleep. I told Jonathan that I had seen the Buddha. "I know," Jonathan said. I asked him how he knew, and he replied, "Because you had a beautiful smile on your face when you were meditating. You looked so calm and quiet. Then you made a mudra and lay down to take a nap, still with that great smile."

"Yes," I said, "Buddha showed me that, and asked me to practice it with him."

Months later, I was in my house by myself in the middle of the night. I lay down on the bed to meditate. Then my door of the bedroom opened very quietly and a lady walked in. She looked both Asian and Caucasian, and her face was very peaceful and beautiful. Her long black hair went all the way to the ground. She had on a long black robe and was barefoot. She walked up to me without any noise. She looked down at me and said, "Don't worry, Jie, everything can be better. After tomorrow, everything will be much better." I didn't know who she was, but I didn't feel scared.

Since that dream, my life changed for the better, and everything went much smoother. I got my green card, as well as one for my wife and my son. I bought my own house. Life was still hard, but I felt much better after that dream.

In January of 1994, a few months after the dream, I went back to China. It was the first time I had been back since I left. In Beijing I went to the Bai Yu temple, the Temple of White Clouds, which is the center of Taoism in northern China. There I bought a picture of the Buddha of Guan Yin. She was one of the best and closest students of the Buddha, and in China is thought to help people in their everyday lives. The picture looked very familiar to me, but I couldn't remember where I had seen her before. I brought the picture back to Seattle and left it in my office. I looked at her almost every day. One day I remembered where I had met her before. She was the same lady from my dream.

I understand that these three dreams are symbolic of my life in the United States. God, Buddha, and Guan Yin came to my dreams and brought positive changes to my life, because I had good karma. I now have a good life here and good relationships. I have been filled with feelings of harmony and peace, and have a new hope for and understanding of life. And all of this started in 1949, when I met the great Buddhist monk at Da Cheng temple.

Why Bagua Is Needed Today

I strongly believe that traditional Chinese culture, including Bagua, is needed by the people of the world. War, famine, the destruction of the environment, greed, and selfishness are all symptoms of this imbalance. Life is lived too quickly in the Western world, causing a lot of trouble. Too many people have chronic injuries, pain, and emotional difficulties from the super-fast pace of life today.

The earth stands now at a crossroads—we have an opportunity to choose a path to peace, health, and harmony for the entire world. Or we can choose a different and destructive path. The only way the world can move in a positive direction is if we gain greater respect for and understanding between different countries and cultures. And as individuals, we need to learn how to make better lives for ourselves, because individuals are the basic foundation of country and culture.

Traditional Chinese culture has a lot to offer both individuals and the world. Perhaps the most important principles it offers are balance and moderation. For example, Confucius says that if you don't do enough, you won't get what you are trying to do. But if you do too much, you may waste much of your work, and trouble is often the result. Too much or too little—neither can help you to reach all of your goals in life. But by strying in balance, life can be fulfilling and rich, and you can enjoy the things that life can truly give us.

Any way you look at it, balance and moderation are the most important principles of traditional Chinese culture. Confucius talks about achieving balance among people. Lao Tzu's system describes how to achieve balance between Yin and Yang, between people and the natural world. Chinese Buddhism seeks a balance between the physical body and the spirit. Chinese Taoism discusses the balance between our present and future lives. This philosophy is a treasure that the Chinese culture can offer to the entire world. And Bagua is a part of that treasure as well.

Bagua offers a time-tested and effective method for people to regain balance. And as people develop better balance, the whole structure of society is strengthened. Without good balance, you cannot help others even if you want to. Good balance in the individual is the foundation for good balance in the family, the community, and the world. With good balance come natural feelings of love and appreciation for life and oneself.

If you truly love yourself, you will naturally have the capacity and the desire to help others achieve balance, too. But without that feeling inside you, even the best of intentions will often fail. The study of Bagua, Taiji Chuan, Hsing-I, Shaolin, chi gong, calligraphy, medicine, or any of the traditional Chinese cultural arts are great ways to understand and attain balance in your life.

Learning Bagua can be of great benefit to both the individual and the society. There is great potential for Bagua in the United States as students make a thourough study of the art. People can learn Bagua, develop good balance, and, as they learn, they can also help Bagua to develop in modern society. They benefit each other. Bagua gives something to people, but people also can give to Bagua. This book is part of giving Bagua to people, but it also gives people an opportunity to give back to Bagua and, through this, to everyone.

Chapter 1

The History of Bagua Zhang

Bagua Zhang appeared in China around the close of the sixteenth century, at the end of the Ming dynasty and the beginning of the Ching dynasty. This was a special time of great change in the history of China and had two important characteristics.

First, the whole social system was in turmoil, and the people had lost their feeling of safety. The government of the Ming dynasty was under control of the Zhu family, who were of the Han ethnic group. At that time the population of China was about 95% Han, and the other 5% was composed of fifty-five minority groups, one of which was the Manchu. The end of the Ming dynasty was extremely corrupt, and the Ching government was able to take over the country. The Manchu minority group controlled the Ching government, and for the Han people, this was a deep and painful hardship. They thought they had a responsibility to protect and save Chinese culture, and many of them sought to overthrow the Ching dynasty and restore native Han rule. As a result, the Chinese people had a strong need to defend themselves, and from this turmoil emerged the great development of Chinese martial arts.

The second important characteristic of this time was that China had a rich and strong system of culture long before the Ming dynasty. This included history, philosophy, morality, medicine, chi gong, martial arts, calligraphy, painting, literature, architecture and engineering, opera, and gardening. This culture gave the martial arts a rich and deep background to develop from.

With traditional Chinese culture "meeting" the rule of the Ching, the stage was set for the martial arts to flourish, and they gained a new importance and status. It was an especially fertile time to develop a new martial art, and it is from this background that Bagua Zhang developed—a material art that was not only extremely effective, but one that was very deeply a product of Chinese culture and thought.

Bi Cheng Xia, Father of Traditional Bagua Zhang

The founder of modern Bagua Zhang is Dong Hai Chuan, who lived from 1796 to 1880. According to legend, he learned his technique from a Taoist master named Bi Cheng Xia. There is a long history of Bagua Zhang before Master Bi Cheng Xia, which is in need of further study, but we consider his Bagua to be the foundation or root of modern Bagua. Bi Cheng Xia practiced Bagua that had been developed by Taoist hermits who lived in harmony with the natural world. This Bagua was passed on for many generations before Dong Hai Chuan first learned it from Bi Cheng Xia. It is important to understand that the Bagua of Bi Cheng Xia is considered to be "traditional" Bagua, as he and his Taoist brothers focused their efforts on how to live a long and vital life, which is a Taoist way of thinking.

Modern scientists have determined that a human being's natural lifespan should range from one hundred to one hundred and fifty years. But most people pass away in their seventies, eighties, and nineties, and only a very few people live over one hundred years of age. Only two people in the history of the modern world have lived to be over two hundred years old. People cannot achieve the kind of long life they deserve because the stress of modern life is very hard on human beings. But Master Bi Cheng Xia and his Taoist brothers showed us that people could live a long and healthy life through Bagua Zhang. This ability is much more important to people than self-defense. It's true that some people do need to defend themselves, but everyone needs health, longevity, and vitality.

In Master Bi Cheng Xia's Bagua, the focus was to practice and strengthen internal chi to support a long and healthy life. Bi and his brothers lived in the natural world, not the world of man. They stayed away from people and didn't have much to do with society. But they still loved their country and its people, and they had a deep feeling of wanting to do something to help them in any way that they could.

In contrast to Master Bi Cheng Xia, his descendants Dong Hai Chuan and Cheng Ting Hua lived not as hermits but in society. They were more focused on a practice that could provide self-defense, teach good morals, and help people live together well. This is a more Confucian than Taoist way of thinking, and their Bagua is considered to be "modern" Bagua. Both Bi's traditional Bagua and the modern Bagua of Dong Hai Chuan and Cheng Ting Hua work to help people, and show a strong responsibility to society and morality. Modern Bagua is simply a development of Bi Cheng Xia's Bagua in a new time.

We need to understand and practice both types of Bagua. Studying Dong and Cheng's modern style of Bagua will lead you back to understanding the traditional Bagua of Bi Cheng.

The traditional Bagua of Bi Cheng Xia is made up of at least two parts. One part is called Xing Ming Shuang Xiu, or the ability to control your mind and thinking. Xing is like putting a collar and leash on a monkey, or a bridle and bit on a horse. You concentrate on letting your spirit be empty and letting the "monkey mind" quiet down. After you become quiet and calm, you practice with Ming, which means that you will naturally begin to feel the energy of your body, which can become very active. This is an example of how the Yang begins to emerge from the deeper Yin. You want to control this feeling and not let it go, so the energy that arises can be transformed into chi and spirit. This is the beginning of nei gong, which is an advanced part of traditional Chinese Taoist chi gong.

The second part of Bi Cheng Xia's Bagua is the external movements. This part of the practice includes the circle walk, the mother palms (including the single palm change), ching gong, and the sword form.

The Bagua that Dong Hai Chuan learned from Bi Cheng Xia was somewhat different from what Liu Bin passed on to Liu Xing Han and Master Wang Wen Kui. Parts of modern Bagua practice are influenced by techniques from different styles of Chinese martial arts, particularly Chinese wrestling. But the Bagua practices of Bi Cheng Xia, Dong Hai Chuan, Cheng Ting Hua, and others all have the same root, which is the circle walk and single palm change.

Dong Hai Chuan, Founder of Modern Bagua Zhang

Dong Hai Chuan was the founder of modern Bagua. There are many stories about him, and some of these stories have special interest for us in understanding modern Bagua.

Dong Hai Chuan Meets Master Bi Cheng Xia

Dong Hai Chuan was very interested in martial arts and started learning them when he was young. When he was about twenty, he started traveling the country to visit and study with various martial arts masters. At that time, he was a very good student of the Lohan martial arts.

One day when Dong Hai Chuan was walking in the mountains, he met a thirteen-year-old boy who was walking around a big pine tree. Dong asked him, "What are you practicing?"

"Oh, this is the Bagua," the boy replied.

"What do you mean by Bagua?" Dong asked.

"Bagua is martial arts."

"I don't think so," Dong said. "Your movement looks so slow and simple. Do you want to practice with me?" This, of course, was a polite way of challenging the boy.

The boy agreed.

Dong Hai Chuan worked very hard trying to catch the boy, but the boy was so limber and so fast that Dong couldn't touch him. After a while he became so tired that he gave up.

"OK, you are better than me," Dong said. "I want to learn this from you."

The boy said, "I cannot teach you, I am still just a student. If you do want to learn the Bagua, you should talk to my teacher."

So the boy introduced him to his teacher, a master of Chinese Taoism named Bi Cheng Xia. Bi was his family name and Cheng Xia was his special Taoist name, which means the beautiful clouds in the mountains.

Bi Cheng Xia asked Dong many questions about his life, particularly his martial arts background. He then decided to teach Bagua to Dong. Dong stayed with his teacher in a small village in Jiu Hua Shan, or Nine Flowers Mountain, in An Hui province. He studied from the master for three years.

Then Bi told Dong, "You need to go back to a normal life, to help people. You cannot stay here with me your whole life. The people need you, and you need your own life." Dong Hai Chuan left, went to Beijing, and started working for the emperor's family, teaching Bagua.

What Became of the Taoist Masters?

In a small village near Nine Flowers Mountain, an old story was passed down for many generations. It was said that three masters of Taoism lived in a cave on the mountain behind the village. Every night they would practice martial arts by walking around a big pine tree. The masters were very friendly to the people, so the people liked them. Nobody knew how old they were, but some townspeople believed they were each over one hundred years old, even though they looked like they were in their sixties or seventies. One person in the village had known the masters as old men when he was a little boy; now he himself was an old man, with children and grandchildren, and still the masters were there—so they must have been quite old. Bi Cheng Xia was one of the three masters, and the other two were his brothers in Taoism.

One day they told the people in the village, "After we have passed away, please seal off the cave entrance and don't tell anybody." Since that time, the story of the three masters of Taoism continued to be passed down in this village, but no one went to open the cave.

In 1966 the Cultural Revolution broke out in China, and the whole country was in chaos. People were confused and acting crazy, and many sad things happened during this time. People were encouraged to destroy anything that was old or traditional, and so some young farmers in the village decided to open the cave. When they did, everybody was shocked: the three masters of Taoism, including Bi Cheng Xia, were still sitting in meditation position with their palms pressed together. One of the masters was facing the now-opened mouth of the cave, and the other two were sitting at either side of the mouth of the cave looking across at each other. Their faces looked very much alive, but their clothes disintegrated at the touch. The bodies of these masters had been around for perhaps 150 years, and these men were known to be over one hundred years of age before they passed on, but their faces and bodies did not look decayed. In fact, except for their clothes, they looked like they were still alive and meditating.

This astonished the townspeople. They took the bodies of the three masters and burned them. This is a very sad story, but it also tells us that the story of Dong Hai Chuan's teacher is true. We know that Master Dong Hai Chuan studied Bagua from Bi Cheng Xia in the small village on Nine Flowers Mountain. Second, we know from this story that the Bagua Zhang martial arts have a special relationship with Taoism. Third, we realize that Bagua not only teaches people special techniques of self-defense but also helps people achieve vitality and lead exceptionally long lives.

In 1986, Master Huang Wan Xang journeyed from Beijing to the village in Nine Flowers Mountain. He found the cave still there, now over-grown, and of course there was nothing left of the Taoist masters. Time had changed everything.

Dong Hai Chuan in Beijing

Dong Hai Chuan believed that he could continue studying, testing, and developing Bagua Zhang in Beijing. He could also find the best students to teach there. He believed that he could do something with those students to help the Chinese people. But first he needed to find a job and a place where he would be able to continue to practice. Dong heard that the Su Wang family was looking for servants, and he decided to get a job there. The Su Wang family was closely connected to the imperial family, so they had a lot of influence and power in Beijing. Working for them would give Dong the safety and influence he wanted, so he could better teach and develop Bagua—it was like he was looking for a big shade tree that could shelter him.

At that time, families would only hire eunuchs or castrated people. This was a big problem for Dong because he was not a eunuch and he didn't want to be castrated (ouch!). But he did want the job and, fortunately, Dong had strong chi and had learned special exercises to strengthen his sexual organs, which enabled him to retract his genitals into his body. In traditional Chinese chi gong this is called Ma Yin Tsang Xiang, or "horse sexual organs withdrawing exercise."

This name requires a bit of explanation. A male horse's sexual organs are usually retracted into the body. When the horse is aroused they come out, but they are protected inside the body most of the time. Ma Yin Tsang Xiang teaches people how to do this using their chi. It takes a lot of skill and practice to get to a high level of internal chi before you can learn to do this.

From this story, it is clear that Dong had unique abilities and had learned a very high level of chi gong. He had unusual control over his body, which is considered a part of the traditional Bagua of Bi Cheng Xia. Dong could protect himself from a powerful strike or kick to the groin, but he could also make himself look like a eunuch. Thus he was able to fool the Su Wang family into hiring him to work in their palace.

Dong Hai Chuan worked in the teahouse of the Su Wang family. Every day he boiled water and made tea for everyone. He looked normal and acted normally, so no one knew that he was a very skilled martial arts master. Su Wang liked the martial arts very much and invited many masters of different martial arts to visit his home. They would talk about and practice martial arts every day. Su Wang himself was a great martial arts master.

In the time of the Ching dynasty, there was a tradition for the emperor and his family to invite martial arts masters to show their arts. Many of the best masters would be asked to teach the men of the emperor's family and would be hired as bodyguards. For example, Emperors Kang Xi and

Chian Long were both great martial arts masters. One day they held a big martial arts competition hosted by the family of Su Wang. The master Sha Hui Hui beat everybody. Sha Hui Hui was also the leader of the martial arts masters in Su Wang's home.

Su Wang was very happy, having enjoyed the competition very much, and wanted some tea. He looked around and asked, "Where is the tea?" Dong Hai Chuan quickly came with the tea. Master Su Wang drank the tea and asked him, "What is your name? How long have you been working for me here?"

"My name is Dong Hai Chuan," he answered, "and I am new, I only started recently."

Su Wang said, "There are so many people here, and I am in the middle of them. How did you get through the crowd so quickly?" Dong Hai Chuan didn't respond, and so Su Wang asked him again, adding, "You should tell me the truth. You practice martial arts, don't you?"

"Oh, yes," said Dong Hai Chuan, "I know some martial arts."

So Su Wang asked other people how Dong had gotten through the crowd so quickly. Everybody said they didn't know because they were watching the competition, but they thought it was strange that he could do that.

Su Wang asked Dong again, "How did you do it? You know I like martial arts."

So Dong Hai Chuan said, "I just jumped into the middle from the outside."

Su Wang said, "Oh, you have a very high level of ching gong. What kinds of martial arts do you practice?"

Dong said, "I practice Bagua."

Su Wang said, "What is Bagua? Does anybody here know the martial art Bagua?" But nobody had heard of it. Su Wang asked Dong, "Please show us this Bagua."

When Dong Hai Chuan showed everyone Bagua, they were shocked! They had never seen anything quite like it before. Su Wang asked Dong Hai Chuan to practice with Sha Hui Hui. Now, Sha Hui Hui practiced external martial arts, and Dong Hai Chuan beat him.

Su Wang was very happy. He asked Dong Hai Chuan to be the new leader of his bodyguards. From that point on, more and more people knew that Dong Hai Chuan was a great martial arts master.

Master Dong's Ching Gong

The following stories show how the ching gong of Bagua was passed down over generations. Ching gong means "lightness skill," and is a special chi gong skill of making the body very light so the person can "super jump" or nearly fly.

The root of ching gong is internal chi. At first you need to do special exercises to learn how to build, control, and use internal chi. After that, you need special training in how to use internal chi to jump higher and faster.

A story about Dong shows us that ching gong was a part of Bi Cheng Xia's old Bagua. One day in the forest, Dong was talking about Bagua, and the students asked him about ching gong. He replied, "Ching gong is not very easy to learn. You should first learn the foundation part and make it very strong. You have a long way to go before you'll be ready to learn ching gong."

At that moment a bird flew by. Dong jumped up into the air and caught the bird in his hands. When he opened his hand to show the students, the bird was standing on his palm. It tried to fly off but couldn't move. Dong was using his chi gong skill to keep the bird in his hand without grasping it. This story again shows us that Master Dong had a very high level of both ching gong and chi gong skill, and that the two were working together. The better your chi gong, the more easily you can develop the skill of ching gong. But chi gong is the root—nobody can do ching gong well without good chi gong skill.

Master Cheng Ting Hua used to have great ching gong skill as well. In 1900, when Cheng Ting Hua fought with German soldiers, they shot him after he had jumped onto the roof of a house and was running away. I will tell you more of that story later in this chapter.

Master Liu Bin, one of the best students of Cheng Ting Hua, also had good ching gong. He was the guard of a wealthy family in Beijing. One night he brought along his young students, the fourth-generation Bagua masters Li Yan Chin, Liu Shi Kui, and Wang Wen Kui. They asked Liu Bin about his ching gong skill. Liu Bin wouldn't tell them, so they kept asking him, "Please, just tell us a bit. How did you learn it?" Master Liu Bin said, "I don't know ching gong," but the students kept asking him. Then, all of a sudden, he disappeared! The young students looked around, and there he was, up on the second floor! Liu Bin to them, "You kept bothering me about ching gong, ching gong. Well, here is ching gong!" And with that, he jumped back down to the first floor.

His son, Liu Shi Kui, became the leader of the fourth generation after Liu Bin died, and he knew ching gong very well. Back in the 1950s, he was working for the National Center for Sports and Movement. He was taking care of the cauldron, boiling water and making steam to help heat the building. One day a young worker made a mistake: the pressure of the steam got too high, and the cauldron was in real danger of blowing up. Master Liu Shi Kui jumped up on top of the cauldron and turned off the relief valve. This cauldron was very big, maybe eight to ten feet high. But he just jumped up to the top. Before that, nobody knew that he was a Bagua master.

Years before, the government had come to his house and said, "Are you the person people call Bagua Liu? We have heard that he is a great martial arts master, and we want him to come and teach." Liu Shi Kui told them, "That isn't me, that was my father. He never taught me Bagua." They noticed that there was a sword and a Bagua knife sitting in the corner of his house, and they asked about them. Liu said, "They were my father's, but nobody wants them anymore. If you like, you can have them." But after the incident with the cauldron, people knew that he was a great martial arts master.

Dong Hai Chuan and the Power of Internal Chi

The master Sha Hui Hui was so angry after being beaten by Dong Hai Chuan that he left the Su Wang family home and quit his job. But in the back of his mind, he was thinking about how to get revenge on Dong.

One night Dong was meditating in his room when Sha Hui Hui and his wife entered through a window. Sha Hui Hui had a sword and thought he would have his revenge. But when he swung down at Dong's head, the sword cut through the bed. Dong wasn't there anymore. Sha Hui Hui was scared and surprised—where was Dong? Then Sha Hui Hui and his wife heard Dong srying very softly, "I am here." When Sha Hui Hui turned around, he saw Dong standing behind them. Sha Hui Hui was very surprised—how did he move so fast? Dong told him, "You are a bad person. If you want to challenge me, do it face to face. Get out of here, I don't want to see you any more." Sha Hui Hui understood that Dong could kill him easily if he wanted to because his martial arts skill was so much better. So Sha and his wife left.

We can see from this story that Master Dong had a very high level of internal chi and Bagua martial arts skill. It also shows us that when Dong was meditating, he was able to have a very quiet spirit with great concentration, and he was also able to be very sensitive to his environment. His awareness was very strong, both inside himself and around him. This is a very high level of chi gong development. A strong awareness inside yourself and around you is the root of the external movements of Bagua martial arts.

Master Dong and Guo Yun Shen

Another story about Dong Hai Chuan describes how a lot of people came to see him after he became famous in Beijing. They wanted to learn Bagua, and various martial arts masters came to challenge him and test their skills against him. One day a Hsing-I master, Guo Yun Shen, came to visit Master Cheng Ting Hua and said, "I know that you are the best student of Dong. I would like to practice with you first." The principle of Hsing-I is "Xian Fa Zhi Ren," which means, "I go to you first." This requires a short explanation. When a martial artist wanted to test himself against a well-known master, it was customary to challenge one of that master's top students first; if you couldn't beat the student, you had no business even bothering the master.

Master Guo struck out at Cheng Ting Hua using Beng Chuan, which was his favorite movement and which he had used to defeat many people. Cheng Ting Hua moved very quickly and Master Guo completely missed Master Cheng and instead smashed the doorframe. Cheng just smiled and laughed. "You cannot touch me," he said. "I don't think you are good enough to practice with my teacher. But if you want to visit my teacher, I can introduce you to him." And so Cheng introduced Master Guo to Master Dong.

They had a big meal together. While they were eating, drinking, and talking, Dong said, "I understand that you want to practice with me. I think that is a great idea. But you are a great master of Hsing-I already. We have no reason to hurt each other. How about this way? Here are your chopsticks and I have my chopsticks. You try to touch me with your chopsticks. I will just protect myself with my chopsticks. Let's see what happens!"

So Master Guo agreed. They practiced for a long time with the chopsticks. Master Guo couldn't touch Master Dong. Everyone around them was very excited and surprised to watch the two great masters practice together with chopsticks. Then Master Guo stopped and laughed. "Oh yes," he said, "You are a great master. I can understand that now. I can't get inside your guard." Master Dong said, "I have never met somebody like you, with such a high level of martial arts skill." They became close friends after that and learned from each other. Guo showed Master Dong Hsing-I, and Dong showed Master Guo Bagua. This story also shows that Master Dong had a big and merciful heart. He always paid attention to different types of martial arts and continued to learn new things to help the development of Bagua. Since his time, each generation has continued to explore the relationship between Bagua and other martial arts, developing and integrating the best parts from other systems into the Bagua system.

That is why, from Cheng Ting Hua's generation on, there are movements from Hsing-I that have been absorbed into our style of Bagua. For example, the form of Twenty-Four Movements of Five Elements, Three Levels begins with the pattern of Pi, Beng, Tsuan, Pao, Heng. These are the foundation movements for Hsing-I, which have been developed and integrated into this form.

Cheng Ting Hua

Because Master Dong and his students lived in Beijing, their Bagua practice was adapted to the needs of the society they lived in. Since the end of the eighteenth century, China had experienced a lot of hardship, many difficult changes, and much uncertainty. It was a dangerous time, and people needed to be able to defend themselves. Therefore, Master Dong's Bagua emphasized self-defense and helping others, and it absorbed a lot of knowledge from Chinese martial arts. All of the masters felt they had a responsibility to help and protect the people and the country. The master who best exemplified this was Cheng Ting Hua.

Cheng Ting Hua was born in 1843, in Shen county of Hebei province, and died in 1900. When he was twelve or thirteen years old, he came to Beijing and learned how to make glasses. He opened a shop in the area of Hua Shi, where he made and sold them. The Hua Shi area is located south of the Chong Wen Men, or the Gate of Chong Wen, which is a part of the south district of Beijing and nearby Tian Tan Park (Heaven Temple Park).

Tian Tan Park is very close to the Tian Chao area, the central working-class quarter of the south district of Beijing and a center for the "pop culture" of the time. Different kinds of martial arts and wrestling demonstrations were going on there all the time. We called Tian Chao the special place of "crouching tiger, hidden dragon." The movie of the same name uses the same traditional Chinese idea. It means that a place can look very normal, but if you look more closely you'll find many great masters of martial arts and wrestling, and a high level of skill in many of the practitioners.

Cheng Ting Hua would teach his Bagua in this area, which the people called Cheng Bagua, or the Bagua of the south district of Beijing. The Chinese name is Nan Cheng Bagua (South District Bagua). Cheng Ting

Hua's Bagua has its roots in Dong Hai Chuan's Bagua, but Master Cheng absorbed and was nourished by the public culture of his time and place, especially the popular martial arts Hsing-I and wrestling.

Master Ti En Fang, who is ninety-two and the oldest of the fifth generation of Bagua masters, told me that Master Cheng Ting Hua had written poetry.

> *The Bagua palm is a special martial art*
> *It comes from the heavens*
> *If you start when you are young, you are lucky*
> *The most important foundation for Bagua is the circle walk.*
> *You should pay attention and practice the circle walk*
>   *your whole life, and*
> *You can gather a long and healthy life, as heaven and earth.*

This shows that Cheng Ting Hua inherited the most important principle of Bagua Zhang from Dong Hai Chuan—that the circle walk is the most important and best exercise. The whole system of Bagua Zhang is built on this foundation. Whether you are a young student or an old master, you should maintain circle walking practice your whole life.

The function of the circle walk is very magical—more magical than people think. That is why Cheng Ting Hua said that Bagua Zhang comes from heaven, and can give you as long a life as heaven and earth (which means basically forever). On this point, Dong Bagua and Cheng Bagua are in close agreement.

The Development of Cheng Bagua

A special characteristic of Cheng Bagua and one of its most important principles is that it doesn't have jumping movements, or Cuan Beng Tiao Yue. Instead, it uses Ai Beng Ji Kao, which means being close to your attacker and using your body. A second special characteristic of Cheng Bagua is "Suo Xiao, Mian Ruan, Chiao, Ai Beng Ji Kao." Suo Xiao means you hold your chi and energy inside and make small movements. Mian Ruan means "relaxed and soft." Chiao means "ingenious." Taken together, this means that first, the attitude of a Cheng Bagua master is very humble all the time—he doesn't show off with his strength and skill. Second, if he needs to defend himself, he will be balanced inside and his physical body will be very relaxed. Third, the movement of the Cheng Bagua technique is small and fast. Fourth, the Cheng Bagua master is able to get close to the opponent quickly. Fifth, he uses his own body most of the time to move the attacker's root. Sixth, the technique for movement is very ingenious and unique.

This means that in case you need to protect yourself, you should be close to the attacker, use your whole body to move the other person's root, and let them fall down. This comes from traditional Chinese wrestling.

People who practiced Cheng Bagua said, "Bagua Jia Jiao Ge Ge Bai Rao." This means that if you use techniques from Bagua and wrestling, you can beat anybody. Master Cheng was a great wrestler before he studied Bagua from Master Dong. A number of Cheng Bagua masters of the third, fourth, and fifth generations were strong wrestlers before studying with Master Cheng. For example, the two famous fifth-generation Cheng Bagua masters Han Wen and Han Wu were also great wrestlers—especially Han Wu, who said, "When you are fighting with an attacker, you need to move close to him by moving quickly in a spiral. Don't move straight in." His grandson, Master Han De, is the leader of the sixth and seventh generations of Cheng Bagua masters.

Cheng Ting Hua was the most important person in the development of Bagua Zhang from an esoteric Taoist martial art into a public Chinese martial art. Since his time, the Bagua Zhang martial arts have been more popular with the people. The average person can see and understand that it is a special martial art. Just like an immortal coming down to earth, Cheng Ting Hua's Bagua is a bridge between the mysterious Taoist arts and the public martial arts.

Master Dong Hai Chuan had many students during his life. More and more people wanted to learn Bagua Zhang from him, especially when he was older. Most of the time he let Cheng Ting Hua, his senior student, teach the younger students. They were officially students of Dong, but Cheng taught them. For example, Master Liu Feng Chun was the youngest student of Dong. He was a glassmaker and made beautiful glass flowers for women's hair. People called him "Cui Hua Liu"—Liu was his name and Cui Hua means "glass flower." Most of his Bagua was learned from Cheng Ting Hua. He paid attention to the single palm change for many years, and over time became a great Bagua Zhang fighter.

Another example is Hsing-I master Zhang Zhan Qui (1864–1948). He was the head of the police in Tian Jin City. One year he came to Beijing looking for criminals. He went to visit Cheng Ting Hua and asked for his help, because Master Cheng was a famous master and knew many people in town. Master Cheng helped Zhang Zhan Qui to find the criminals, and they became good friends. Zhang Zhan Qui told Cheng that he wanted to learn Bagua from him. Cheng replied, "We are good friends, like brothers, so I cannot be your official teacher. But I can introduce you to my teacher."

Zhang Zhan Qui then became a student of Dong. But most of his Bagua was learned from Cheng. This shows how Cheng was a humble person, not out to impress people. He would show Zhang the Bagua, but since they were friends he didn't want to claim that he taught him. He wasn't trying to become famous or sound important to others; he just wanted to help people learn Bagua, because in his mind he was always thinking about how to develop it. Bagua was more important that his ego.

One day a young man came to Beijing from Shandong province and found Cheng Ting Hua's home. He wanted to learn Bagua. This man was big, strong, tough, and also very poor. He had walked all the way from Shandong to Beijing, about eight hundred miles. Cheng Ting Hua talked to him and found out he was a nice person and had a good martial arts foundation. He let him stay in his home for over a month to teach him the foundations of Bagua Zhang and to take care of him. This guy had a big appetite and would eat five pounds of bread and two hundred pot stickers for lunch. Finally Cheng told him, "Right now you have a good foundation for Bagua Zhang, but you need to go home to practice. If you stay here, it is hard for me to feed you." The man was very happy, and he returned to Shandong. This story shows that Cheng Ting Hua was willing to teach Bagua to people who were sincere, whether or not they were rich or famous. He felt he had the responsibility to develop and pass on the Bagua Zhang that he learned from Master Dong, adding his personal experience to it along the way.

Cheng Ting Hua and the German Soldiers

The year 1900 was the blackest time in the history of China. The Ching dynasty was corrupt and weak, unable and unwilling to govern the country well. Because of this, the Eight-Nation Alliance (composed of the United Kingdom, France, Germany, Italy, Japan, Russia, Austria-Hungary, and the United States) invaded the country. They wanted to get natural resources, open Chinese markets to trade, and exploit cheap Chinese labor. All of these countries had armies stationed in Beijing and were causing terrible damage to the city. They burned the great gardens of Yuan Ming Yuan, destroyed the imperial palace, and killed, looted, and raped as they went. Cheng Ting Hua was sad and angry. He wanted to protect his country and the dignity of his people.

One day, after he came out from his home in Beijing, German soldiers stopped him in the street and tried to question him. Master Cheng didn't understand German, but he felt that foreign soldiers had no right to stop him. "Why are you here in my country," he asked them, "stealing our things, killing, and destroying?" So Master Cheng and the Germans ended up fighting. Master Cheng wasn't fighting for himself; he was trying to protect the dignity of the Chinese people. He beat many of the German soldiers, weaving through them, and they couldn't catch him even as he was killing them. They said, "This guy is magical!" and called for more soldiers. Master Cheng thought it was time to escape, and he jumped onto the roof of a nearby building. As he was running away, his queue (a long ponytail hairstyle) got caught in the roof tiles, so he had to jump back down before jumping back on the roof again. This gave the German soldiers time to shoot him.

Master Cheng Ting Hua died to protect Chinese dignity and respect. He was the best example of a Chinese martial arts master, having lived his life at a high moral standard. He was generous to people and helped everyone. After Dong Hai Chuan, he was the most important person in the history of Bagua Zhang martial arts. His spirit will live forever in the minds of the Chinese people.

Liu Shui Bagua and Zhuang Gong Bagua Zhang

Cheng Ting Hua had many great students, and they continued to develop Bagua Zhang into a modern, nineteenth century Chinese martial art. Master Liu Bin—one of the top students of Master Cheng—and his Bagua brothers Li He Ting, Ji Feng Xiang, Liu Zhen Zong, and Guo Feng De had a special impact on the development of Bagua Zhang after Master Cheng.

After Cheng Ting Hua, the Bagua of the south district split into two schools. One was called Flowing Water Bagua, or Liu Shui Bagua. Cheng Ting Hua's sons, Master Cheng You Long and Master Cheng You Xin, developed this school. The other school is Zhuang Gong Bagua, which means Strong Root (like a tree's root) Bagua. Master Liu Bin and his Bagua brothers developed this school.

What are the differences between these schools?

To give you a simple answer, the biggest difference between them is that Liu Shui Bagua emphasizes very smooth, effortless, and beautiful movements that are light and quick, while Zhuang Gong Bagua pays more attention to building a strong root in the body through lots of slow circle walking. Zhuang Gong Bagua also has some special forms and exercises that can help to build a much stronger root in the body. The two schools teach many of the same forms and in the same order, but they have a different feeling to them.

What accounts for this difference? Since they both came from the Bagua of Cheng Ting Hua, how did they change? There are a couple of different reasons. First, different people have different backgrounds, different temperaments, and their own experiences and goals, and this affected how each school developed. Liu Shui Bagua emphasizes speed and dynamics more than power. Zhuang Gong Bagua emphasizes the power and rootedness of the movement more than speed. But both emphasize the development of great health and vitality.

I think that all things, even very small things, are more complicated than people think. Liu Shui and Zhuang Gong Bagua show two different profiles or angles of Bagua Zhang, but both are related to the essence of Bagua Zhang. If you look very deeply, Liu Shui Bagua isn't against and doesn't exclude good rooting, but it just doesn't emphasize it as much. In the same way, Zhuang Gong Bagua doesn't exclude fast motion or a smooth flow. Without a good root you cannot develop much real speed, and without being able to move quickly, you cannot fully express your root and strength. The elements of speed, smoothness, and root are all important in developing a complete Bagua martial artist. If you lose any of these elements, you lose the true essence of Bagua.

Both Liu Shui Bagua and Zhuang Gong Bagua are part of Cheng Bagua. Liu Shui Bagua is like the flower of the tree, while Zhuang Gong Bagua is like the root, trunk, and branches. Without the roots and trunk, there is no flower. A flower is beautiful to look at and highly valued. But I think that in general, it is better to pay more attention to developing strong roots and a healthy trunk and branches. Beginners especially should pay close attention to developing a good root and good basics, because to have a big tree you first need strong roots and a strong trunk. It takes years of practice, but after you develop a strong root and great balance, then you can work on speed and quick changes of technique. But when you get older, you may not be able to keep your speed even if you still want to. The only way for you then is to return back to root practices.

In both your life and practice, things come full circle. Everything comes from the root, and everything returns to the root. That is why Master Ti En Fang, who is ninety-two years old and a fifth-generation Bagua master, always asks his students to pay more attention to the circle walk. And after age seventy, he focused his own practice on the circle walk and single palm change, srying, "That is good enough for me to practice." This principle—of beginning and ending with roots—is not just for Bagua, but is the way for everything in the universe, big and small, plain and beautiful.

Liu Bin and the Nan Cheng Wu Lao

Master Liu Bin was also known as Kuin Chuan. His exact dates of birth and death are unknown, but he lived from about the 1870s until the 1930s. People called him Nan Cheng Bagua Liu, or South District Bagua Master Liu. He was the founder of the Nan Cheng Bagua School. He was a general in the army of the Ching dynasty before 1900, but after Master Cheng was killed, Master Liu quit his job because he was so sad and angry at the government for not doing all it could to repel the invaders. He just stayed in his home and wouldn't work. He focused his time and energy on teaching Bagua. He and the masters Ji Feng Xiang and Wang Dan Ling were invited to teach at the national martial arts school in Hebei province. Master Liu also worked as a bodyguard in Beijing. He specialized in the jiu jie bian, which is the hardest weapon to use. It is made up of nine sections of metal connected with links and is about six feet long. You can fold the weapon up small or wrap it around your waist, so it was convenient to carry. It can be used in a hard and stiff way, like a staff, or in a soft and flexible way, like a snake. You need special techniques, strength, and a lot of chi to use this weapon. Liu Bin also knew ching gong very well.

Master Liu and Masters Li He Ting, Ji Feng Xiang, Liu Zhan Zong, and Guo Feng De were called the Nan Cheng Wu Lao, or the Five Old Masters of South District Bagua Zhang. Master Ji Feng Xiang was called Ma Gan Ji, or Long Whip Ji, because he used to have a business that sold whips and was very good at using them as weapons. He was also a very good doctor of Chinese medicine and was an *I Ching* master. Master Li He Ting was a master of the nei gong (advanced chi gong) of Bagua Zhang. Master Liu Zhan Zong, the father of Liu Xing Han, knew many of the different forms and weapons very well. He was also a businessman who made good money to support the research of Bagua Zhang. Guo Feng De was a very humble person, very quiet and nice, with good internal balance. He practiced all of the forms very well. These masters would get together to practice and research Bagua almost every day at Liu Bin's home. Liu Bin was the leader of the group, and many special forms were passed down from them.

They included:

- Twenty-Four Movements of Eight Animals
- Twenty-Four Movements of Five Elements, Three Levels
- Sixty-Four Movements of the Four Directions of the Bagua Circle
- Sixty-Four Movements of Eight Trigrams
- Continuous Circle Walk of Nine Palaces
- Twenty-Four Movements of Eight Fists, Eight Elbows, and Eight Palms
- Sixty-Four Movements of Bagua San Shou (or free-fighting set)
- Dragon Long Staff Form
- Middle Staff of Five Elements
- Short Staff of Seven Stars
- Lian Huan Sword
- Chun Yang Sword
- Ping Xing Sword
- Double Sword of Dragon and Phoenix
- Turning Sword
- Big Curved Bagua Sword with Turning Wrist Form
- Bagua Spear Form
- Bagua Guan Dao (or halberd)
- Tse Wu Yue or Double Crescent Knives Form

All of these were developed or codified by these five masters. I believe that some of these were passed on from Cheng Ting Hua, and the five masters developed the others based on what they had learned from their teachers. They also researched the relationship between Bagua and the philosophy of the *I Ching,* and made special herbal formulas to treat injuries and the effects of overtraining.

The school where Master Liu Bin taught was in the Tan Tong area of Heaven Temple Park. The third generation of this Nan Cheng Bagua group was significant for three reasons: First, they passed on the treasure of Bagua Zhang from Master Cheng Ting Hua and continued to develop and teach it. Second, they strengthened the South District Bagua school. Third, many people came to Liu Bin to practice and develop their Bagua skills.

The Four Factors for Learning

In traditional Chinese martial arts, whether it is Bagua, Taiji Chuan, or another kind of martial art, you need four factors if you want to develop what you have learned, become a master of a martial arts style, pass on the knowledge correctly, and move the martial art to another stage of its development. These four factors are money, friends, time, and place.

You need money because you need to be able to practice and support your research. You need friends who share your interests and background, because practicing and researching by yourself makes it hard to learn about martial arts. Confucius said that when three people walk on the road together, each of them can always learn something from the other two. This means that people learn better together—they can help each other focus, share ideas, and practice. A traditional Chinese srying goes like this: "With a group of people, if each person takes one branch of a tree, together they can make a bigger fire than any one person can." The factor of time means that you need to live in a time when you have access to a great teacher who can pass on the treasures of the martial arts. Place means that you need to live in the right place to be near a great master; you also you need a special cultural environment, or "cultural nutrition," that can support your understanding of what you are learning.

The Nan Cheng Wu Lao are a good example of this. They all had good businesses and money. They studied with Cheng Ting Hua and became close friends. Master Liu was the leader, but they practiced together all the time to develop their skill. They lived from the 1870s to the 1930s, so they had a chance to study with Master Cheng, who had inherited the treasure of Bagua Zhang from Dong Hai Chuan. They lived in the south district of Beijing, around Heaven Temple Park, a special area for Chinese public culture. From their cultural environment, they learned from Shuai Jao, Chinese medicine, the *I Ching* philosophy, and other kinds of martial arts in order to understand and develop Bagua Zhang. Living in such an environment makes it easy to learn more.

Liu Xing Han

Master Liu Xing Han practicing with Bagua Jian, or Bagua sword

Master Liu Xing Han was born in 1910 and died in 2000. His other name is Ping Shan, given to him by Master Liu Bin back in 1930.

Ping Shan's father, Liu Zhen Zong, was one of the Nan Cheng Wu Lao. Liu Zhen Zong was a very close friend of Master Liu Bin and learned from him. He had his own business, made good money, and used it to support the practice and research of the Wu Lao every day. Over time, he and Liu Bin became Ba Xiong Di, which means "brothers from different families." This ceremony is part of traditional Chinese culture. It takes place between very close friends who want to be recognized as brothers, even though they have different parents. In the ceremony, two (or more) people say, "We were born on different days, but we want to die on the same day." They are in life together. They also exchange paperwork with each other's names and birthdays.

Over time, Liu Zhen Zong's Bagua rose to a very high level. Liu Bin and Ji Feng Xiang decided to let him "come in the door" and become an official student of Cheng Ting Hua, but Cheng Ting Hua had already passed away. So Liu Bin and Ji Feng Xiang organized a Pai Wei ceremony for Liu Zhen

Zong, in which he officially claimed Cheng Ting Hua as his teacher and became a third-generation Bagua master.

When the Nan Cheng Wu Lao practiced and researched Bagua in Liu Zhen Zong's home, Liu Xing Han always came to watch and listen. At that time he was eight or nine years old. Master Ji Feng would sometimes give him notes from the research, which was written in poetry form. He would tell him, "Keep this, it is very important. Never lose or forget this, and it will benefit your whole life!" That is why Master Liu had so much knowledge of Bagua. He was very lucky and took good care of what he received. Back in 1979, when we were working on the first Bagua book together, he used these old notes and what he had learned as the basis for the book. When he was ten, Liu Xing Han began learning Bagua Zhang from his father. Then his father said, "It is time to send you to your uncle, Liu Bin. His Bagua is the best. You should learn from him." So, in the 1920s, Liu Xing Han became the youngest and last student of Master Liu Bin.

Group picture of some of the fourth generation masters.
Master Liu Xing Han is on the left, holding the Bagua Jian

Liu Xing Han then started his own business in southern Beijing. But he continued to practice Bagua at Tian Tan Park with Master Liu Bin. In the

1940s he started to "open the door" and have students of his own. His first student was Liu Jing Liang, who lived in the city of Kun Ming in Yunan province. He was a professional Bagua teacher, certified by the government as a Bagua teacher at the highest level. He is the vice president of the Wushu Association of Yunan province. In 1980 he competed in a national wushu competition, and he was given a special award for his performance of the Bagua Guan Dao. Also, in 1983, he was given an award from the national government for being an outstanding Bagua Zhang teacher.

During the Cultural Revolution, traditional Chinese culture was nearly destroyed. Master Liu Xing Han continued to practice, but in secret. He knew he was taking a big risk, but he did it anyway, and he continued to research Bagua theory and saved the old documents that he had. At the same time, Master Liu Shi Kui, Liu Bin's son, had been safekeeping the notes from his father's research. The people of the Cultural Revolution discovered this and told him to give them all the Bagua paperwork so they could burn it. Liu Xing Han heard this was happening and went quickly to Liu Shi Kui's home. "Older brother," he said, "give me the paperwork and let me save it." Liu Shi Kui replied, "Doing this is very dangerous, are you sure?" Liu Xing Han said, "I know it is dangerous, but I don't care. This is my mission."

During the Cultural Revolution, Master Liu Xing Han continued to practice and research the art of Bagua Zhang. He also prepared to write a book on Bagua. He believed that someday the Cultural Revolution would be over, life would go back to normal, and people would be interested in learning Bagua Zhang once again.

The Tomb of Master Dong Hai Chuan

Around 1910, the Bagua masters of Beijing made a memorial stele out of a large rock tablet and placed it in front of Dong Hai Chuan's tomb. On the tablet they inscribed his name, dates of birth and death, and his poetry on why to learn Bagua and how to become a master.

The rock tablet said, "Today, we make a big memorial stone for Master Dong Hai Chuan. We want to tell the people the Tao of Bagua Zhang. We want to tell the people how to become a Bagua master, and tell you the morality and justice of Bagua Zhang. We want people to understand the principles of Bagua Zhang, too. For the people who want to learn, they should understand the goal of Bagua. This is working for people and the country, not for yourself; Bagua people should step forth and defend the people and the country. Most important for Bagua people is to try very hard to be a moral person. After that, pay attention during practice to your spirit and internal chi. Make your spirit and energy strong and balanced. These two things—morals and practice with spirit and chi—are much more important than the techniques. This is the heart of Bagua Zhang."

The tomb of Master Dong Hai Chuan

Poetry from Master Dong's tomb

In this poem, there are twenty Chinese words that are important to understand, for each has an important meaning to Bagua students.

Hai	Fu	Shou	Shan	Yong
Chiang	Yi	Ding	Guo	Ji
Chang	Ming	Guang	Da	Lu
Tao	De	Jian	Wu	Ji

These twenty words mean: "The benefit of Bagua exercise is to give you a long and a nice life, like the sea and the mountains, and to give you good training and a strong spirit, so you can work for the country and strengthen it. Make the mainland of China a bright place, with high morals and good life."

These words are also used to name special students of Bagua. For example, Master Dong Hai Chuan was the first generation of Bagua, so his name came from the first of the twenty words. Master Yin Fu's name came from the second word. Master Liu Xing Han's Bagua name, Ping Shan, came from the fourth word of the poetry. "Shan" means mountain, and "Ping" means peaceful and balanced. Together, the meaning is that there is good balance inside and outside, and that his life should be as long as a mountain's. My Bagua name is Yong Guang, which is from the fifth word of the poetry. Yong Guang means "help to develop Bagua so it can continue forever."

More History of Bagua Zhang

There are of course many other masters of South District Bagua Zhang. We have mentioned some of them here, but this history section is focused on just the head of each generation. In our second book, we will tell the history of many of the other masters and talk about their philosophies on Bagua and life.

Chapter 2

The Essence of Bagua Zhang: Theory and Cultural Roots

Bagua, the *I Ching*, and Chinese Culture

How exactly is Bagua Zhang related to Chinese culture? To understand this, you need to understand that the source of Chinese philosophy is the *I Ching*.

What does *I Ching* mean, exactly? "I" means change or, to say it more deeply, the change of Yin and Yang. The *I Ching* tells us that everything is made up of Yin and Yang, whether it's as huge as the universe or as small as an atom. And everything is changing, because the relationship between Yin and Yang is always changing. Sometimes they are in relative balance, but usually they are out of balance; sometimes they are working together, and sometimes they clash. They are mutually dependent on one another: if there is no Yin, the Yang dies, and if there is no Yang, the Yin dies.

The word "Ching" means classic book. So, in total, *I Ching* means "classic book of changes." Why is it considered a classic? Because it describes the function of everything: it is considered the root of the way of Chinese thinking and culture. Of course, the masters who developed the Bagua system would follow the Chinese way of thinking, and they would describe it using the terms of the *I Ching*. It was a part of how they thought, so naturally it would influence how Bagua developed.

The *I Ching* philosophy is embodied in the Bagua map, a template of eight symbols called trigrams. The Bagua map describes the Chinese method of thinking about the universe. (See illustration on page 32.) First, the Chinese people believe that the essence of the entire universe is both matter (or substance) and emptiness. Second, Yin and Yang, and the mutual changes between them, are what underlies everything. They are the central points of the *I Ching* system. Because Yin and Yang create and clash with each other, things don't stay the same but constantly change. For a short time Yin and Yang will be in balance, but then they will change again and be unbalanced.

The matter that makes up the universe can be divided into five elements: metal, wood, water, fire, and earth. The five elements are the foundation of the universe and are related to Yin and Yang. For example, earth and water are Yin and fire is Yang. Metal is more Yang than Yin. Wood is more Yin than Yang.

From the five elements we move on to the four directions or four corners, which describe the condition of human beings living in the universe. The universe is all around human beings, just like the four directions. Wherever you go, there is still north, south, east, and west. We exist within the universe, which is three-dimensional like a sphere. This sphere is called San Cai, which means "sky, man, and earth." Human beings stay in the middle, between the earth and the sky. We are a part of the universe.

Human beings have the initiative and potential to understand the universe, and by understanding it, to create harmony within our spheres of influence. Bagua Zhang movements, especially the circle walk, single palm change, walking on the Bagua map (tracing a pattern of the map with your stepping pattern), and using the body to make the map (tracing the map with the movements of your entire body) teach you through direct experience about the meaning of the *I Ching*. You could say that Bagua movements are "talking" about the *I Ching* by using special body language.

One of the main functions of Bagua Zhang practice is to develop and create good balance between the Yin and Yang of your body. For example, you practice the circle walk and all movements going in both directions, Yin and Yang. Doing any movement, your body is constantly in the process of going back and forth between Yin and Yang. You are making good balance between the Yin chi and the Yang chi of the body, between the Yin channels and Yang channels of the body. You are creating balance between the five Zhang organs (Yin) and the six Fu organs (Yang), between the chi (Yang) and blood (Yin), between Ying (Yin; nutritional energy) and Wei (Yang; protective energy), between the physical body (Yang) and spirit (Yin), and so on. In short, when you practice Bagua Zhang, the Yin-Yang relationship is always in your movements and in your thinking.

Yin and Yang, therefore, are the most important principles for the generation, development, and practice of the art of Bagua Zhang. Where did the Yin-Yang concept come from? From the *I Ching,* of course. The *I Ching* tells people that everything in the whole universe is simply a combination of Yin and Yang. The essence of the universe is Yin and Yang. How, then, could Bagua be outside of the principles of the universe?

The *I Ching* describes the objective laws of the development of the universe, of everything within the universe—from emptiness to fullness, from the lowest stages to the highest stages, from the simple to the complicated. These are the principles that the Bagua masters used to create and develop the Bagua system.

Because the universe is constantly changing, Bagua Zhang is based on the concept of change, and that is why Bagua practice includes so many "changes," or movements altering your direction. From the circle walk to the single palm change and the eight mother palm changes, from the twenty-four movements form to the sixty-four movements form, from palm forms to weapons forms, the entire Bagua Zhang system is based on the *I Ching* principle of change.

Bagua Zhang and its movements are organized in harmony with the eight trigrams of the Bagua map. All of Bagua Zhang's movements can be divided into eight types, as described by the eight animals—lion, snake, bear, dragon, phoenix, rooster, chilin, and monkey. The nature of the Bagua Zhang movements is based on the natures of the eight animals, and the animals themselves are examples of the nature that each Bagua trigram expresses. For example, the lion is majestic, the snake is smooth, the bear is stable, the dragon is dynamic, the phoenix is like a tornado, the rooster is like a fire, the chilin has very good balance, and the monkey is quick and limber. Thus, the bear movements in Bagua Zhang emphasize stability, the monkey movements emphasize quickness, and so on.

Illustration of the Bagua map, elements, and animals

It can be said that developing harmony, or creating balance within change, is the true aim of the *I Ching*. The philosophy of Lao Tzu is centered around harmony between man and nature, the idea that humans should have love, appreciation, and respect for nature, and understand that they are a part of nature. The philosophy of Confucius is centered around harmony between people, that humans should have love, appreciation, and respect for people, and understand that they are a part of society. Both of these concepts are focused on harmony and love.

Although Bagua Zhang itself is relatively new, the philosophies that have guided its development are the same as the *I Ching* and are at the core of the Chinese way of doing and thinking. Some people think that Bagua Zhang is only for fighting, that it is just a martial art. But the practice of Bagua Zhang helps to develop internal balance within the person who practices. A person with good internal balance will naturally be a good person, a good friend, and a good member of society. Thus, the practice of Bagua Zhang can help develop harmony in the manner of Confucius.

Bagua Zhang helps you to feel your body, your movement, your chi, and your spirit. In this way, people practicing Bagua will naturally become more sensitive to the world around them and feel their connection to nature and the earth. Thus, the practice of Bagua Zhang can help develop harmony in the way of Lao Tzu. Whether it is the *I Ching,* the *Tao Te Ching* (Lao Tzu's book), or Bagua Zhang practice, they all teach the same philosophy—harmony and peace. That is why I think the practice of Bagua is the correct, simple, and useful way to deeply understand Chinese culture.

We've talked about Bagua's relationship with morality, health, medicine, martial arts philosophy, and many other things. But the focus of Bagua Zhang is the individual, the person who is doing the practicing. This idea also comes from the *I Ching,* Lao Tzu, and Confucius.

But what is the key point a person should focus on in practicing Bagua Zhang, if you want to gain all of the benefits? It is to pay more attention to your internal chi and to your internal balance. Focus on this, and you will gain a better understanding of Bagua's morals and philosophy. You will gain better health, long life, and vitality, and you will become a good person filled with love and harmony. That is the main goal of Bagua Zhang practice, and also the main goal of *I Ching* philosophy.

The goal of the person's spirit is a high level of morality. The goals of the physical body are longevity and great health. Love of life and nature is the way to make great harmony. Working together, they help to make the Bagua Zhang practitioner a great person.

Martial Morality (Wu De)

When people think about Wu De, they usually think about a standard of conduct that tells people to "do this" or "don't do that." Of course, this is very important, but Wu De is not a simple set of rules to follow.

The Wu De of Nan Cheng Bagua has a very clear philosophy. The highest stage of Bagua Wu De is seeking and building harmony, which has three levels. First, you need to develop internal harmony. The second level is to develop harmony between yourself and others, your family or community. The third level is to build harmony between yourself and nature, including the earth and the universe. This elevates Wu De from the level of rules to the level of philosophy. A set of rules only works for the situation it was intended for, while a philosophy can function in a new or novel situation. Rules reduce an individual's personal responsibility, while a philosophy places responsibility on the individual. The philosophy of Wu De comes from Lao Tzu and Confucius, who both believed the highest stage of life is harmony.

The second stage of Wu De relates to standards of conduct. Before, in the stories of the old masters and their students, we talked about some of the standards of conduct that students were given. We don't need to repeat the exact rules of conduct; we just want to point out that the root of those rules came from the philosophies of Lao Tzu and Confucius. Both philosophies are very rich and deep, but we want to give a few simple examples of how Wu De is related to each.

For example, Lao Tzu said, "The most wise are like water," because water is usually quiet, balanced, soft, and adaptable. Water is merciful—it brings life and growth when it is in balance. But it also has great power. Lao Tzu also said, "Water is the softest and weakest, but nothing can overcome it."

Confucius said that a moral person would always be a winner in life. If you're a moral person, being "the winner" becomes unimportant in the bigger picture, because you have other goals to achieve. When your goal is harmony, everyone can win, and that is true victory. Confucius also said, "The most moral person should be full of love for others." A major principle of Confucian thought is to understand and forgive.

Young students often need more explicit rules while they internalize the deeper philosophy. But more important than following these rules is understanding why they are good rules and why they help the student learn. Ultimately, the Bagua student develops his or her own personal way to develop harmony, and in doing so the rules become less important.

The third goal of the philosophy and standards of conduct in Nan Cheng Bagua is to make the student a new person. This means that having students improve and develop themselves into more than they were when they started is the central point of Wu De. Wu De is not just talk or theory. Wu De is practice, and that practice changes you. A person who practices Bagua with the right attitude will become a very different kind of person, going beyond just being strong to being a force of goodness and balance for himself and those around him.

Wu De is the soul (the heart) for Bagua students. If you want to learn Bagua (or other martial arts, for that matter), you need to pay attention to Wu De and traditional Chinese morals. This helps with your training. But as you develop, you should be finding out how to apply Wu De to your daily life as well. Every action in life should be filled with the attitude of Wu De, and everything you do is a reflection of your Wu De. Wu De is always the first thing you need to pay attention to, whether you are a student or a master.

The philosophy system of Lao Tzu teaches people how to make harmony with nature. How can we develop that harmony? Lao Tzu gave people an answer to this question: "Wu Wei Wu Bu Wei." "Wu Wei" can be translated as "not doing." "Wu Bu Wei" can be translated as "*not* not doing," or what you should be doing. Together, this means that you should make the right choice to do something, and you should also make the right choice to not do something. Another way of srying this is: make the best choice to do something that can make the best harmony between people and nature, and make the best choice to not do something to harm or ruin harmony between nature and people.

Lao Tzu also said, "Shi Ren Yi Rou, Shi Ren Yi Ruo." The meaning of this is: when you communicate with others, always show people the soft part of you. This is based on the principle of "Rou Ruo Sheng Gang Chiang," that soft things can beat hard things. Lao Tzu believed that if you make the right choices in all things in your life, always show people your softer side, and be kind and merciful, then you can make good harmony with nature and people.

Confucian philosophy provides a way to make harmony with people. How is this done?

Confucius described four ways to make harmony with people. The first principle is Ren Ai. This means you should love people. He said, "If people love each other, we can fill the world with love. We can have peace in the world through love." The second principle is Shu. This means you should understand and forgive. Confucius said, "If there is only one thing to practice for your whole life, it should be Shu. Understand and forgive." The third principle is Xing, which means introspection. You should ask your heart at least three times a day, "What am I doing wrong?" You need to be willing to look inside at your own faults and also at what you are doing right. You should then keep on doing the good stuff and change the bad. The fourth principle is moderation. All of the time, in all things, you should be moderate and stay in the middle—too little or too much of anything can both have a bad effect. To have the best effect, you want to be moderate in your thoughts and actions. For Bagua, we need both philosophies, because even though they are ancient they are also clearly related to our modern times. The ideas and practices of Lao Tzu and Confucius are just as useful today as they were 2,500 years ago.

Although we've talked a great deal about philosophy, we haven't talked much about the rules to follow. The rules are important, but philosophy is the root of the rules. If you understand the philosophy, it helps the rules make sense and you don't just follow them blindly. Philosophy is like the sun—it brings warmth and light to people, nature, and the earth. It supports and nurtures us. When you are practicing Bagua Zhang, you should follow the rules that the teacher sets for you, but try and understand why you are following the rules. Try to see how the rules can help you learn and develop. This is how you unite the rules and philosophy as one.

Bagua Zhang and Traditional Chinese Martial Arts

Bagua is one of the youngest martial arts in China. As it developed, it absorbed lots of nutrition from the whole body of martial arts systems in China. Without the history of traditional Chinese martial arts, there would be no Bagua. Traditional Chinese martial arts are like the mother and Bagua is like the youngest, special son. If traditional Chinese martial arts are like the sky, Bagua Zhang is like a bright star in that sky. Or if traditional Chinese martial arts are like fertile soil, then Bagua Zhang is like a beautiful rose bush.

For example, one of the principles of Bagua is: "Shou Yan Shenfa Bu." Shou is hand or fist, Yan is eyes, Shenfa is body, Bu is stepping. Whenever you practice, you should coordinate your hand, your eyes, your body, and your legs. In this way, you can learn to move fast and powerfully with good balance. Shou Yan Shenfa Bu is a very important principle of traditional Chinese martial arts that Bagua has absorbed.

Another example is the foundation stepping patterns of Bagua, such as Gen Bu, Gung Bu, Pu Bu, Ma Bu, and others, which come from traditional Chinese martial arts. When you are fighting, you use your palms, fists, and elbows, similar to other Chinese martial arts.

At the same time, Bagua is totally different from other kinds of Chinese martial arts. It has its own characteristics and special features. Compared to other martial arts, Bagua Zhang asks students and practitioners to pay more attention to developing morals. Bagua Zhang also places a lot of importance on the cultivation of health, vitality, and longevity. It expects that you should be developing both internally and externally, both the physical body as well as the energy and spirit.

Bagua Zhang has totally different forms from other traditional martial arts. The first characteristic is the special walking practice called circle walking. Doing the walking improves your health, develops strong legs, strengthens your organs and chi, and improves your focus and concentration. The walk includes spiritual practices, chi gong exercise, health cultivation, and martial arts all in one. The form is simple, but its content is deep and profound.

Another characteristic that distinguishes Bagua Zhang is that it emphasizes a lot of body twisting and spiraling. This creates great physical strength and internal chi. It also opens up the channels of the body and greatly improves circulation. In this point, Bagua Zhang has the closest relationship with traditional Chinese medicine of all the martial arts. It is much more closely coordinated with the theory of Yin and Yang, the five elements, Zhang and Fu, the channels, the points, chi, and blood than are other martial arts.

For self-defense, the Bagua Zhang of Liu Bin often uses throwing and knock-down techniques. This lets you protect yourself well without having to greatly damage the other person. This combines effective self-defense with morality, particularly mercy. I call Liu Bin's Bagua a merciful martial art for this reason.

Since the times of Dong Hai Chuan and Cheng Ting Hua, Bagua Zhang has become a rich system with many branches or schools. But even so, the most important principles of Bagua remain the same, for the root and trunk of the Bagua systems are the same. What are these root principles? They are the circle walk and body twisting, the single palm change, the eight mother palms, and other movements. The circle walk and body twisting give Bagua Zhang its unique characteristics. This is similar to the four fundamental forces of Peng, Ji, Lu, and An, which are unique characteristics of Taiji Chuan.

I want to emphasize again that Bagua Zhang keeps a special focus on the spirit. This includes morality, all kinds of balance and harmony, and prying great attention to the cultivation of health and longevity. That is why people call Bagua Zhang an internal martial art.

Bagua Zhang and Chinese Wrestling

Chinese traditional wrestling, or Shuai Jiao, has a long history dating back over 2000 years. Shuai Jiao has been practiced in China since the Han dynasty (206 B.C.–A.D. 220). At that time it was called Jiao Di. In the Tang (700–907) and Sung (960–1276) dynasties, it was called Xiang Pu. In the Ming (1368–1644) and Ching (1661–1911) dynasties, they called it Shao Bo. In modern times it is called Shuai Jiao or Liao Jiao.

Some sports are suited for elite athletes, but many regular people practice Shuai Jiao for fun and to stay in shape. In China it's a very popular exercise, both in the city and in the country. Because there are many regular people practicing Shuai Jiao, there is always a good pool of talent to move up to the professional ranks. At the same time, the professional players raise the standard of performance as they keep developing the game with new techniques, strategies, and training methods. This competitive environment improves the art of Shuai Jiao and makes it a very rich and important part of China's cultural treasure.

Shuai Jiao has influenced all of the Chinese martial arts. Let me give you an example from Chinese literature. In a famous novel called *Shui Hu Zhuan,* written about the time of the Song dynasty, there is a famous story about a martial artist named Ren Yuan and a wrestler named Yan Ching. Ren Yuan was a big, strong man and a fearsome fighter. He had built a Le Tai platform and promised a lot of money to anyone who could knock him off it. Many people tried to defeat him, but they all lost.

Then Yan Ching challenged him. He was not as big as Ren Yuan, but he was strong, handsome, and known for his beautiful skin and the dragon tattoos all over his body. He was also very well trained in Shuai Jiao. When Yan Ching jumped up onto the platform with Ren Yuan, the people said, "He looks so young and small compared to Ren Yuan. I think he may be in trouble." But Yan Ching took off his long robe to show his skin, tattoos, and strong muscles. Ren Yuan quickly tried to grab Yan Ching, but Yan Ching just moved to the side again and again, getting behind Ren Yuan. After a while Ren Yuan began to get angry. He let his chi rise and was breathing harder. He went after Yan Ching again, but this time extra fast and hard, so hard that he was a little off balance. Yan Ching waited until he was really near and then dodged him again. This time he grabbed Ren Yuan by the armpit and inner thigh, lifted him over his head, and threw him off the Le Tai platform. Yan Ching's victory was an example of how beautiful the techniques of Shuai Jiao are.

In more recent history, since about 1960, there have been four main schools of Shuai Jiao—in Inner Mongolia, Shanxi province, Hebei province, and in Beijing. Each school has its own emphasis and special techniques. For example, the Shanxi province school has a very strong Bao Tui or "holding the leg" technique. It has many variations and can be used to throw an opponent, even if the opponent knows it's coming. The Inner Mongolia school emphasizes power, strength, and conditioning, or what is known as Ban Li, natural power. Hebei province specializes in the use of Bie Tze, or controlling the opponent's legs with your legs and throwing him. The Beijing school absorbed many techniques from all three of these schools, making it the Shuai Jiao school of the highest level.

Beijing is a special place for Shuai Jiao. The city has many of the best professional players and the sport has been very popular there for a long time, especially in the southern district, which has the best players. When I was seven years old I began going to Tian Chao, the center of public culture in south Bejing since the sixteenth century, almost every day after my classes to watch the wrestling. At that time the most famous Shuai Jiao master was Master Bao Shan Lin, also known as Bao San. He had an outdoor stage where he and his students would display their Shuai Jiao skills. Everybody had beautiful techniques and could move very fast, especially Master Bao San (who was about forty at the time) and his youngest student, Master Ma Gui Bao. When these two would practice together, their movements were so fast, their bodies so limber, and their techniques so beautiful that it was like watching two butterflies flying together. They left a deep impression on me forever.

A few years ago I saw Master Ma Gui Bao on a Chinese New Year television program, the first time I had seen him since the 1950s. He was much older, of course, but he still had very strong chi and a strong body. He said that he still practices and teaches Shuai Jiao, and he said the sport has a bright future in China. Even today, the south district of Beijing is one of the centers of traditional Shuai Jiao wrestling. There are also places similar to Tian Chiao in the east, west, and north districts of Beijing as well.

Another big reason for Shuai Jiao's popularity in Beijing has to do with the history of the Ching dynasty. During the Ching dynasty there was a special part of the army called the Shan Pu Ying, which was dedicated to protecting the emperor and emphasized Shuai Jiao practice. Everybody who was a part of the Shan Pu Ying was at the highest level of professional wrestling. The Shan Pu Ying was a privileged group that had a great reputation, so there was a lot of competition to be in it. If a family had a son who was accepted into the Shan Pu Ying, it was a big deal, and the whole family—even the whole neighborhood—was very excited and proud. The Shan Pu Ying was a part of the Ching dynasty for virtually the whole period, giving it hundreds of years of development. When the Ching dynasty ended in 1911, many members of the Shan Pu Ying continued to practice and teach all over Beijing, bringing many skills and techniques to the modern Shuai Jiao schools.

Since the south district of Beijing is both a center for Cheng Bagua as well as Shuai Jiao, the two have developed together in a natural way. Like two old friends, they just naturally influence each other in good ways. When two people have lunch together from the same pot, it takes time for them to get used to each other, but gradually each person gains new ideas and understanding. That is why Master Cheng Ting Hua, who was a second-generation Bagua master, as well as many other Bagua masters, was also a Shuai Jiao master. For example, Master Han Wen (fifth generation), Master Han Wu (fifth generation), Master Cui Yu Bin, and Master Men Xian Xiang were all great Shuai Jiao players as well as masters of Bagua Zhang.

And the Cheng Pai Liu Shi Bagua (another name for Liu Bin's Bagua; literally "Cheng style, Liu school Bagua") absorbed and integrated the treasures of Shuai Jiao, including principles and specific techniques. Let me give you an example. Master Wan Yong Shun was a great Shuai Jiao player of the Shan Pu Ying. After 1911, when the Shan Pu Ying was disbanded, he went back to normal life and continued to teach Shuai Jiao. Two of his students, Master Shan Wan San, also known as Shan San, and Master Bao San, were great players of Shuai Jiao in the 1920s–1940s. And Bagua master Han Wen, who was best friends with Bao San and Shan San, was also a professional Shuai Jiao player. Back in the 1930s, Han Wen's brother Han Wu came to Beijing from their hometown in Hebei province. He lived with Han Wen, practiced Shuai Jiao, and also became a great Shuai Jiao master.

Han Wen was also a very close friend of Bagua master Zhang Gou Xiang and asked him to teach Bagua to Han Wu. Zhang Gou Xiang gave Han Wu a very hard test, throwing him three times in a row. And then Zhang Gou Xiang found out that Han Wu was a nice man and liked him. He decided to ask Master Liu Shi Kui to teach Han Wu instead. Because Liu Shi Kui was Liu Bin's son, he had a very high level of Bagua, not only because he practiced hard and long but because his dad was a high-level master. But Liu Shi Kui said, "We should both teach him, but he is under your name." So Han Wu was taught Bagua Zhang by both Zhang Gou Xiang and Liu Shi Kui. After Zhang Gou Xiang left Beijing to travel the country, Han Wu continued to study Bagua from Master Liu Shi Kui.

In the 1940s Master Liu Shi Kui fell on financial hardship and illness, and Han Wu took him to his home, where he cared for him for three years. Liu Shi Kui felt so thankful to Han Wu that he taught him everything he knew. When Han Wu started to learn Bagua he stopped practicing Shuai Jiao, because he wanted to show respect for Bagua and focus his energies on it alone. But the techniques, principles, and spirit of Shuai Jiao left a deep impression on Han Wu that he couldn't forget. As he practiced the Bagua, his Shuai Jiao training had a subtle influence on his practice, and the two forms became united. People think that Han Wu's Bagua is pure Bagua. His movement is very relaxed and soft, like cotton. But inside there is the power of a strong storm.

I studied some Shuai Jiao when I was a boy, and it helped me understand the movements of Bagua when I started to learn it from my teacher Liu Xing Han. I can tell that there is a special relationship between Cheng Pai Liu Shi Bagua and Shuai Jiao. When I started learning Bagua, I felt the similarity but didn't know how to articulate it. But now that I'm a Bagua teacher, I can understand it well enough to talk about it. I would describe the deep similarity between the two arts in terms of four main points: First, Bagua and Shuai Jiao both use Heng Li, or horizontal power. Second, both move along the arc of a circle. Third, both can help you to develop good chi and feel your chi ball around you. In other words, when you practice Shuai Jiao or Bagua you should have the feeling of a ball of energy around your body. Keeping this feeling during practice develops the best balance within your body. It also gives you the best freedom of movement, so you can move very smoothly anywhere, anytime, and in any direction. This is called Chuan Fang Wei movement, which means moving your whole body in twisting and spiraling movements. The meaning of these words is subtle but important. Most martial arts movement is based on going in a straight line. But Bagua and Shuai Jiao movement is based on moving in all three dimensions, in circles and spirals. Bagua Zhang is more powerful than Shuai Jiao in this movement, although both develop it.

Fourth, the self-defense techniques, principles, and spirit of the two are similar. But Cheng Pai Liu Shi Bagua is Bagua and isn't Shuai Jiao. The root is totally from traditional Bagua, the Bagua of Dong Hai Chuan and Cheng Ting Hua. The big difference between the Cheng Pai Liu Shi Bagua and other Bagua styles is that Cheng Pai Liu Shi Bagua has been more open to the entire system of Chinese culture and has continued to absorb "nutrition" from that culture, no matter if it is classic or public culture.

When we say that Cheng Pai Liu Shi Bagua and Shuai Jiao have a special relationship, it doesn't mean that Shuai Jiao can replace Bagua. Bagua is Bagua, and Shuai Jiao is Shuai Jiao. They are different. Or you could say that on the path of Liu Shr Bagua, Bagua found a close friend in Shuai Jiao.

Differences Between Internal and External Martial Arts

There are many differences between internal and external martial arts. In external martial arts, you usually attack your opponent by moving in toward him. You want to get your opponent as quickly as possible. But in internal martial arts, you wait for your opponent to make his move and then you start your movement. Once your opponent has started moving, you move quickly and stay close to him, moving to his side or behind him. Another important point is that for external martial arts, the most important elements are power and speed, and the techniques are usually aimed at injuring the other person. An internal martial arts master is different. He emphasizes getting the opponent off balance or breaking his root. Once you have broken your opponent's root, he will fall down by himself. This also means the internal master doesn't cause as much damage to his opponent (although the opponent could still get hurt by falling down). You could say that the internal arts help you to develop a more compassionate attitude toward others, even while they teach you to keep yourself safe.

Another difference is that in external martial arts your focus is on one part of your opponent's body, usually the point you are going to hit. In internal martial arts you are trying to break your opponent's root, and therefore you're paying attention to the opponent's whole body and movement. In external martial arts, you emphasize using your fists, elbows, and so on. The emphasis is on developing your body into a weapon. In internal martial arts you can use the same weapons, but you emphasize whole body movement. You are more likely to push or "help" someone to fall by using his own strength and movement against him. The internal master doesn't want to win. He just wants his opponent to understand that his attitude is wrong, and that he should change, become a nice person, and stop trying to hurt people. Compared to the external arts, the internal arts are much more merciful.

All of these principles should be a part of your regular practice. In regular practice, the external martial arts emphasize strengthening muscles and building power and speed. The internal martial arts focus on developing the internal chi and balancing the spirit. The internal arts pay more attention to making your body much more coordinated and to Xia Pan, which means building a strong root and balance. This is not just physical balance, but also emotional, mental, and spiritual balance. The external martial arts are more suited to big and strong people, because the emphasis is on beating the opponent. The internal martial arts pay more attention to self-development because they focus on improving yourself on many levels, not just fighting. Fighting is one part, but it is not the most important part.

In Cheng Bagua we use a special phrase to talk about developing strength: "Wai Mian Ruan, Nei Han Gang Bao Zhi Li." This means that your internal chi and external muscles can be as soft as cotton, but both of them can also be as strong as metal. It depends on what you need.

A good example is Uncle Wang Wen Kui, the older brother of my teacher, Liu Xing Han. Years ago in Heaven Temple Park we were practicing Bagua, and at this time Uncle Wang was eighty-two or eighty-three years old. He tried to explain "soft as cotton, strong as metal" by asking me to try to pinch the skin on his back. On a normal person it's hard to pull the skin away from the body, but his skin was so soft and supple that I pulled his skin almost six inches away from his body! And then he said, "OK, try again." Uncle Wang didn't move, but all of a sudden his skin pulled back from my finger like a rubber band snapping back. He did it just with his chi. I tried to pinch him again and I couldn't do it—it was like pinching a rock. Again, he didn't do anything obvious; he was just standing there, letting me do it.

Master Wang's son, Wang Zhen Ting, told me the following story about his father. Back in 1950, Uncle Wang was working for the Beijing post office. It was Chinese New Year, the people had a big party, and they invited Master Cui, who was a master of San Huang Pao Chui (a style derived from Shaolin), to show his martial art. Master Cui was demonstrating with the long spear and at one point he twisted and snapped the spear, breaking it into three pieces. The people said, "Wow, that is great! Ooh, so powerful." Master Cui was very proud of himself.

Then the people said to Master Wang, who was friends with Master Cui, "We know you are a Bagua master. You have been famous since you were young. Show us your art." Master Wang stood up and said, "OK, let me show you the spear too!" The people said, "Why, Master Cui is so good, what can you show us that is better?"

Master Wang started practicing with another big spear. The way he handled the spear made it look like a noodle! He spun it and bent it around his body. And this was a big, strong spear, not a soft one made to bend. A normal person couldn't even break a spear like that over their knee. And after Master Wang practiced, the people asked him, "How do you do that? The strong spear looked like a noodle!" Uncle Wang was very short, even for an older Chinese man, so it was very surprising that he could do this. He just smiled and didn't answer, but Master Cui said, "That comes from the internal chi." And after that, Master Cui stopped demonstrating the spear.

For a great master, the internal chi and the external muscles can be both as soft as cotton and as strong as metal. Master Wang had much more internal chi than I do and much better control of his chi. There are three reasons why he was so good. First, he was one of the best students of Master Liu Bin, who was one of the best students of Cheng Ting Hua, who in turn was one of the best students of the founder of Bagua, Dong Hai Chuan. Master Wang was taught thoroughly by people who had learned the art thoroughly. Second, he practiced Bagua a lot during his whole life. He never stopped practicing Bagua until he died. Everybody in our lineage knows how much he practiced. Third, he and his Bagua brothers were always practicing together and helping each other improve.

The Bagua people in Beijing called people like Uncle Wang "Xia Si Gong." "Xia" means to pay or to spend and "Si Gong" means your own time. This means Uncle Wang and people like him loved Bagua from the heart, and they spent their free time practicing and learning just because they wanted to. Nobody told them they had to practice. Bagua was a main part of their daily lives, so, of course, they got really good.

Bagua Zhang and Traditional Chinese Chi Gong Exercises

The circle walk is related to numerous Chinese traditional chi gong exercises, including:

- Xao Yao Bu Xing Gong, or relaxation and walking exercise
- Tie Dan Gong, or making the middle of the groin as strong as metal
- Shi Liu Duan Jin, or Sixteen Silk-Reeling Exercises
- Xiao Zhou Tian Gong, or Small Heavenly Circle
- Da Chou Tian Gong, or Large Heavenly Circle
- Zhan Zhuang Gong, or standing and rooted meditation
- Wu Chin Xi, or Five Animals
- Yi Jin Jing, or making the tendons and the body strong and relaxed at the same time

All of these forms, including the many traditional Chinese medicine chi gong forms, Taoist chi gong, and Buddhist chi gong, are related to the practice of Bagua. For example, the principle movement of Xao Yao Bu Xing Gong is relaxed walking with special methods of breathing. Tie Dan Gong has many movements that work toward developing and strengthening sexual energy and the sexual organs. Shi Liu Duan Jin has many movements that emphasize the twisting of the whole body, which develops the channels, energizes the organs, strengthens the muscles, and stretches and strengthens the ligaments and tendons. The most important exercise in Xiao Zhou Tian Gong and Da Chou Tian Gong is to concentrate on the small heavenly circles of the Du channel and the Ren channel. The large heavenly circle adds the twelve channels of the body as well. Zhan Zhuang Gong is focused on prying more attention to developing a strong root in the body, so the legs are strong and supple. Zhan Zhuang Gong teaches the legs to be very stable on the ground just like a big tree, as if your feet had roots. Wu Chin Xi is focused on imitating the movements of animals to strengthen people's chi, balance, and strength. Yi Jin Jing is focused on stretching and strengthening the muscles, tendons, and bones.

The most important principle for all chi gong forms is that the breath, concentration, and movements all become one. The second most important principle is that the external and internal elements of the body are strengthened. The external elements include muscles, tendons, and bones, while the internal elements include your body as well as sexual energy, chi, and spirit. Chi and energy are not the same—energy is actually doing something, while chi is something that is stored or ready to be used. When you use the body and chi to do something, that is energy. Chi is a special type of matter. You may be able to feel the chi, but you cannot usually see it unless you practice chi gong and learn it very well. Then you may develop the ability to see the chi. The third principle is that most movements and exercises come from imitating animals and are related to the natural world. All three principles have been integrated into the art of the circle walk and are important to understand when practicing any part of the art of Bagua Zhang.

Here is another great example of how the Bagua is related to chi gong. In China in 1980, Master Bian Zhi Zhong started openly teaching the traditional long chi gong form of Hua Mountain school of Chinese Taoism. Before this, the form was a closely guarded secret. Today, this chi gong form is very popular. The longevity form includes exercises done standing, sitting, squatting, kneeling, lying down, rolling, and crawling. Master Bian Zhi Zhong didn't teach all the exercises, but only taught the sitting, standing, and lying-down ones.

I studied and practiced all three of them with him. From my experience, Nan Cheng Bagua is, in some ways, very close to this longevity chi gong form. We have already talked about how all the movements in Nan Cheng Bagua have a strong twisting of the waist and back and squeezing of the internal organs. In this type of movement we are working on Xia Dan, or strengthening the lower Dan Tian. All of the movements and exercises of the longevity chi gong form also involve twisting the waist and squeezing the sexual organs. The goal of these movements is to strengthen the hormonal and lymphatic systems, and thus strengthen people's immune systems to prevent disease and to maintain and improve health.

Each of the chi gong methods has over a thousand years of history. Bagua Zhang has benefited from and absorbed much of the wisdom of Chinese chi gong practices. Because the old masters of Bagua Zhang were open minded, their system was able to take in and absorb the treasures of the Chinese chi gong systems. Bagua Zhang is an open system, not conservative but progressive. Yet, at the same time, it isn't true to say that Bagua has all the movements and practices that you find in other systems. Instead, by simply practicing the circle walk and single palm change, you can get all the benefits of the other chi gong sets because Bagua develops all these elements simultaneously, not one at a time as in other systems. Bagua is, in this sense, much more efficient. The circle walk and single palm change have all the benefits of the other the chi gong sets, including good concentration of mind, good balance of body and spirit, good internal chi, and good health. But Bagua also has something these other chi gong sets don't have: self-defense. While you are getting healthy, you are also getting prepared to defend yourself (just in case). Nan Cheng Bagua absorbed all the treasures of traditional chi gong and integrated them with martial arts training.

Bagua Zhang and Traditional Chinese Medicine

Traditional Chinese medicine has a history going back more than three or four thousand years. The foundation of traditional Chinese medicine includes the theory of the channels and points, the theory of the internal organs of Zhang and Fu, the theory of chi and blood, the theory of Yin and Yang, and the theory of the five elements. Nan Cheng Bagua absorbed all of the treasures of Chinese medicine and developed them with the circle walk and single palm.

For example, everybody knows that regular walking is an excellent exercise for health. Modern medical research tells us that if you walk for a half hour every day, you can avoid many illnesses, such as heart trouble, diabetes, obesity, etc. Compared to a regular walk, the circle walk is much harder to do but much more effective for developing health and longevity. During the 1970s and 80s, the Sports Research Institute of Beijing conducted tests on two groups of old men. One group had never practiced Bagua. The other group had practiced Bagua their whole lives and included Masters Wang Wen Kui and Liu Xing Han. They had the two groups do the same exercise—twelve minutes of quick walking. Then they measured their heart rates, blood pressure, and skin temperature, conducted blood assays, and more. They discovered that the Bagua group was much healthier in all the tests—they could walk much more quickly, their heart rates were slower, and their blood pressure was more regular. The Bagua masters of old took the most basic thing—walking—and improved it to create the circle walk. It gives many more benefits than normal walking, and combines, in a brilliant way, health, vitality, and martial arts.

I've talked before about the circle walk and single palm change. I would like to repeat myself a little bit, to explain how the Bagua masters integrated traditional Chinese medicine into Bagua Zhang. As one example, you should keep the top of your head up during the circle walk. This is called Xuan Ding. At the same time, you need to draw back your chin a little, straighten your neck, and let your body relax and sink from the shoulders down. This is called Zuo Shen and has many effects. First, it opens up the Bai Hui point, located in the middle of the top of your head. All of the Yang chi of the body meets at this point. If it is open, you can absorb more Yang chi from the sky. Second, it straightens your spine and body, so that the Bai Hui point, the upper Dan Tian, middle Dan Tian, lower Dan Tian, and Hui Yin point all lie in a straight line. This connects them, so chi can move up and down much more smoothly. This also helps to bring nutrition to all of the organs and the entire body in a balanced way.

When walking, the thighs, knees, and ankles should gently touch each other and be squeezed together. The function of this is to squeeze and open the three Yin channels of the foot, which are the spleen channel, liver channel, and kidney channel. It strengthens the three corresponding internal organs: spleen, liver, and kidney. It also opens and regulates the three Yang channels of the foot, which are the stomach, gall bladder, and urine bladder channels. This, in turn, strengthens the corresponding internal organs: stomach, gall bladder, and urine bladder. Whether you're practicing the circle walk or single palm, your arms do a lot of twisting, coiling, and extending. These motions open and affect the three Yin channels of the hands, including the lung channel, the pericardium channel, and the heart channel. This in turn strengthens and regulates the corresponding internal organs: the lungs, the pericardium, and the heart. The same motions also stimulate and regulate the three Yang channels of the hand, including the large intestine channel, the triple burner channel, and the small intestine channel. This strengthens and balances the large intestine, small intestine, and the interconnection between the three levels and all the organs of the body.

We have talked about the Xuan Ding and Zuo Shen above. Another function of the Xuan Ding and Zuo Shen is to open up the Ren and Du channels. During all of the movements and exercises, your body (and especially your upper body) is always twisting, untwisting, coiling, and uncoiling, which opens up the channels. Traditional Chinese medicine has the theory that the Ren channel is related to the six Yin channels of the body and regulates the Yin chi of the body. And traditional Chinese medicine calls the Ren channel the sea of Yin channels of the human body. This means that when the Yin channels have an excess of Yin chi, the Ren channel can store and gather that excess Yin chi. When there isn't enough Yin chi in the six channels, they can absorb Yin chi from the Ren channel. Also, the Du channel and the six Yang channels of the human body have a similar relationship. That means the Bagua movements can adjust the Yin chi and the Yang chi of the human body through the Ren and Du Channels. So all of the Bagua movements are working for all fourteen channels, including the twelve regular channels and the extra two channels of Ren and Du. The fourteen-channel system communicates with the viscera and extremities closely, connecting the five Zhang organs, the six Fu organs, the extremities, bones, skin, muscles, and tendons, as well as the five sense organs. This means that Bagua movements work on developing and strengthening all of the systems of the human body.

For the circle walk, the entire sole of your foot should slide gently on the ground. This massages and stimulates the points on the bottom of the foot. And by stimulating these points, you stimulate and benefit the entire body and its energy. For the single palm posture and single palm change, you should be twisting your body a lot. It should be constantly coiling and uncoiling. This action massages and strengthens the muscles, bones, tendons, ligaments, joints, channels, circulation, and the internal organs. It develops pretty much everything, but especially the circulation of chi and blood.

Of course, the Nan Cheng Bagua system has many different forms, including palm forms, weapons forms, and many others. But all of these exercises use the same principles as the circle walk and the single palm, and thus all have the same benefits for health. All of the Bagua movement exercises should be practiced in both directions on the Bagua circle. The counterclockwise direction is Yin, while the clockwise movement is Yang. When you change from the Yin to Yang direction, or Yang to Yin, it regulates and balances the Yin and Yang of the body.

So we can say that Nan Cheng Bagua Zhang absorbed all the treasures of traditional Chinese medicine and integrated them within the exercises.

How Bagua Zhang Has Influenced Other Arts

I've described how all aspects of Chinese culture have influenced Bagua Zhang. But Bagua has also, in turn, had its influence on Chinese culture and on many other arts. Chinese opera is one great example.

Beijing opera is a treasure of traditional Chinese culture, both classic and public, and is famous throughout the whole world. Beijing opera is based on four major parts: singing, speaking, performance, and martial arts. Bagua helps opera performers to develop all four of these skills. First, Bagua helps you develop strong chi and body energy to practice and perform in the opera, which takes a lot of stamina and strength. An opera can last three or four hours, with two performances a day. Some of the longer, more historical operas have many "chapters" and can take up to a month to perform, plrying for three or four hours a day. These serial operas are called Lian Tai Ben Xi and are often performed around the Chinese New Year. It takes incredible mental and physical stamina just to remember all the parts, and even more energy to perform well night after night. It is this kind of strength that Bagua Zhang helps opera performers develop.

Also, Bagua practice improves your breathing capacity, which supports your singing and speech. You learn to sing or speak from your Dan Tian, just like when you practice Bagua. And you can develop strong physical energy and good concentration to support your performance. Great performers have "presence," or vitality in their energy and spirit. Bagua Zhang helps to develop that same vitality. Also, Bagua Zhang gives you beautiful martial arts techniques, good balance, better speed, and improved concentration, which are all important elements of martial arts performance in Chinese opera.

The great master of opera Tan Xin Pei was considered the ancestor, or founder, of modern Beijing opera. Of course, opera existed before him, but he brought big changes and improvements to many aspects of opera. In many ways, his development of opera is similar to Dong Hai Chuan's development of Bagua. For example, Tan Xin Pei excelled in plrying the general or the hero. His martial arts performance in opera was astounding, almost unbelievable. This was because he studied martial arts when he was a child. When he played the young hero Shi Xiu in the opera of Cui Ping Shan, he gave a beautiful performance with the knife. This was because he studied the Liu He Dao form. He also used some of the Liu He Dao form in his performance. He didn't practice Bagua, but from his example we can see the special relationship between martial arts performance in an opera and traditional Chinese martial arts.

Master Tan Xin Pei's stepson and student Yang Xiao Lou was the heir to the legacy of Tan Xin Pei. Tan Xin Pei was equally good at all four roles, which was very unusual. That was why he was considered the king of opera. Yang Xiao Lou, who lived from 1870 to 1935, was also very good at all four roles, but particularly excelled at the roles of general and hero. He learned from many of the older opera masters, especially from Tan Xin Pei, and was a big influence on all of the actors who came after him. He also was a Bagua master, having studied with Cheng Ting Hua. During his acting career he adapted his Bagua martial arts to use in the opera. For example, he would wear a long heavy robe and a large hat when he performed, and on his back were four flags that stuck out behind him. He also wore shoes with big lifts so that he would look taller, and he performed with a long spear. All this made it hard to move around, but because of his Bagua training he could move very easily and well. When other actors practiced with Master Yang they would get very tired and have a hard time keeping up with him. But Master Yang could move very quickly and smoothly, and it was no wonder he was such an influence on the opera.

One of the elements of Beijing opera is quickly turning from one direction to another. It is difficult to change directions quickly and with balance while maintaining a good posture, but this is important for the feeling of the opera. Today they still talk about "Yang style turning." He was so good at it that people would applaud every time, surprised and happy to see such a high level of skill. People liked the Yang style of turning, but they didn't usually know how he did it. Master Yang developed this skill through the practice of Bagua, especially the Zhuan Jian form, a treasure of the Nan Cheng Bagua system that includes many turns using a very long Bagua sword. After Master Yang retired, he moved to a Taoist temple, practiced meditation, and lived there until he died.

Here's a third and final example of Bagua's influence on opera. There was a great and famous Beijing opera actor named Mei Lan Fang. He was born around 1897 and died around 1963. He often played the role of a beautiful lady and, in particular, the wife of the general, who would be played by Yang. In one of the most popular operas, the woman does a dance with double swords. Mei Lan Fang was known for performing the most beautiful sword dance, which he had developed himself. But the roots of the form are from Bagua. Mei Lan Fang learned Bagua from Cao

Shi Chuan, a third-generation Bagua master. Master Cao was also Mei's bodyguard for many years. That was how Mei was able to learn the Bagua sword. Because of Mei's real martial arts experience, he could make the sword form look both real and beautiful at the same time.

There is a particularly famous opera that they both played in, called *Ba Wang Bie Ji,* or *Farewell My Concubine.* At the end of the opera, we find that the general Ba Wang (played by Yang) lost the war. Before he kills himself, he and his wife (played by Mei) are talking. The general tells his wife he doesn't want to go home, is ashamed, and wants to die. But he tells her to go home because she doesn't need to die. The wife says, "Yes, my dear, but I want to show you my dance before I go." So she shows the general her sword dance, which makes him feel very happy, if only for a moment. At the end, she kills herself and then he kills himself. It is a very sad but beautiful story. And the sword dance comes from the Bagua double sword form. The actors Yang and Mei played these roles together many times. It was a very popular opera and remains famous even today. And one of the things that helped them create great performances was their Bagua training.

A number of students have told me how their Bagua practice has improved their ability in other art forms as well. For example, my student Jason has been practicing Hung Gar Gong Fu for many years and is quite good at it. Since he began studying Bagua with me and practicing the circle walk and single palm change every day, his Hung Gar friends tell him that he has better balance, movement, speed, and focus. Cort Gay is a good soccer player, and during the seven years he has studied with me his Bagua has greatly improved. He tells me that before soccer games, Bagua exercise gives him good energy to play. He says he also has improved movement and balance during games, especially when quickly changing direction. When his soccer friends ask him why he's gotten so much better at these skills, he says it's because he practices Bagua Zhang.

Another student, Richard Shapiro, plays in a rock band. After six years of training in Bagua, he has a much better feeling when plrying music. He says making good music is similar to practicing Bagua—when everything starts working right, you can begin to feel the pulse and flow of the energy. If the whole band catches the feeling, the audience will start to feel it too. Great music needs a lot of feeling when it's played.

Several of my Bagua students also study calligraphy from me. They say Bagua practice helps them have better calmness and balance inside themselves as they do calligraphy. They can feel the Yin and the Yang change with the brush movements.

Another Bagua student was a very good skateboarder. He only took a few classes with me, and learned just the basic circle walk with single palm and You Shen (or turning-back palm), but even this helped him to become very strong and to gain much better balance for skateboarding.

The performing arts are all about being able to project and communicate feeling, so it's natural that the practice of Bagua Zhang would benefit students in this way. And by improving their bodily strength and balance through Bagua, athletes will certainly improve their performance. But Bagua can benefit everyone. My opinion is that with better focus you can do anything better, whether it's basketball, tennis, soccer, or going to work.

Chapter 3

How to Practice Bagua Zhang:
Circle Walk and Single Palm Change

Before you begin your practice of Bagua, there are some general principles you should understand.

You should have a teacher who has a deep and rich background in Chinese culture, not just in martial arts. Such a teacher will point you in the right direction to understand the special relationship between Bagua Zhang and Chinese culture, including philosophy, morality, Chinese medicine, chi gong, and martial arts as well as calligraphy, history, literature, poetry, and folk customs.

You should understand that the purpose of practicing Bagua Zhang is not just for fighting. Rather, it is a path to a good life, to becoming a special person who has high morals, to developing good internal balance, and to making harmony with people and nature. Bagua will help you develop excellent health and, in case you need it, self-defense power. But learning to fight is not the main goal.

You should be prepared to practice Bagua Zhang for your whole life. This is a challenge for many people. By accepting this challenge you develop perseverance, or the ability to keep doing something consistently. This is important for Bagua practice but is also important in almost anything you want to do.

Proceed systematically. Nobody can be a master by practicing for one day, one year, or even three years, just like you can't gain three hundred pounds by eating one meal. You have to pay attention to regular practice and have a reasonable, balanced practice regimen.

Pay close attention to and spend most of your time on the foundation practices. The roots of Bagua Zhang are the circle walk and single palm change, but there are other foundation practices that are also important. These include the Twenty-Four Movements of Eight Animals; the Twenty-Four Movements of Five Elements, Three Levels; the Twenty-Four Movements of Eight Fists, Eight Elbows, and Eight Palms; the eight mother palms; the rooted standing and one-leg standing exercises; Bagua meditation; and many others. You should remember over your whole life what Confucius said: "Wen Gu Er Zhi Xin." This means that you always have a better, deeper understanding when you review and practice the old things you have studied.

After you have a good strong foundation, and if you can keep up your practice of the basics, then you are ready to learn more. But please remember that the purpose of studying more is to help you understand the foundations more deeply.

Lao Tzu said, "Yi Sheng Er, Er Sheng San, San Shang Wan Wu." This means, "All of the universe, the ten thousand things, are all made from one." Lao Tzu also said, "From Wu Ji [emptiness] to Tai Ji [the origin of Yin and Yang]; Tai Ji to Yin and Yang; Yin and Yang to everything, the universe. Then, finally, back to Wu Ji." When you practice Bagua Zhang after you are fifty or sixty years old, you should return to practicing the foundation, particularly the circle walk and single palm, or even just the circle walk. That is good enough for cultivating health, which is the principle of everything.

It is important to understand that Bagua Zhang is both old and new. In one sense it has its roots in the treasures of traditional Chinese philosophy, morality, medicine, chi gong, martial arts, and Shuai Jiao, as well as in the culture and customs of Beijing. At the same time, Bagua has integrated and transformed all of these treasures into the art we know as Nan Cheng Bagua Zhang. It has absorbed the essence of all these things, so that studying Bagua can lead you to a better understanding of them. Of course, you need to pay attention to all of the elements of Chinese culture that are within Bagua; you limit yourself if you think of Bagua as just a martial art. Without this broader perspective, you won't be able to fully express the spirit of Bagua Zhang. You should remember this point during your whole life. You should first become a good person, with internal balance and harmony with other people, nature, and the environment. This is the greater purpose of real Bagua Zhang practice.

This raises the question: how can you understand all these arts without serious practice in each of them? The answer is to make sure to find a good teacher who has learned the Bagua system well. Your teacher will know how to point out the connections between Bagua Zhang and its related arts. How does the teacher know? Because of the rich development of the art of Bagua, the masters of old had a deep understanding of these things and integrated them into their Bagua. So it is already in there, waiting to be discovered by good students.

This shows how important it is to find the best teacher. Great teachers can do more than teach you—they can lead you to directly find the essence of Bagua Zhang. A great teacher should be like a clean mirror, showing you the treasures of Bagua without distortion. You can say that the Nan Cheng Bagua Zhang system is like a magical mountain with hidden treasures, and the Bagua teacher is the mountain guide, helping you find these treasures.

Principles of the Circle Walk

The circle walk contains the core or seed of Chinese philosophy, morality, medicine, and chi gong, and also is the source and the foundation of the Bagua martial arts system for the following reasons:

- The circle walk reflects the most important principles of traditional Chinese philosophy, such as Yin and Yang.

- The circle walk reflects the highest stage of Chinese traditional morals, such as moderation and balance.

- It reflects the most important principles of Chinese traditional medical theory, relating to the internal organs, channels, points, chi, and blood.

- It reflects the highest stage of traditional Chinese chi gong, as in Xing Ming Shuang Xiu, or combining movement and quiet, Dong Jing Je He, or combining the internal and the external, and Nei Wai Jei He, or combining spirit, thoughts, chi, and movement.

- There is a big difference between humans and animals. People stand and walk on two legs. When people are standing and walking, their hands are free to make tools, weapons, and many other things in life. Over time this affected our brains, giving it new opportunities to grow and develop. And so human beings became what they are today—walking on the legs alone and standing truly upright are very important to being human. But in modern times, human beings have started to lose the talent and ability to walk well. They drive, they take the bus, they fly, they sit in front of the TV or computer—all these things cause people to lose their walking ability, their leg strength, and health. The walk is the most important and useful exercise to cause people keep their health and exercise safely. The masters of Bagua found out, over many generations, that walking was very important for people, and what was true thousands of years ago remains so today. They changed the regular walk to the circle walk, which is much more useful, in many important ways, for improving health.

- If you compare all of the different forms and styles of Bagua, the circle walk is the simplest exercise. But it is also the most beneficial exercise. Just like Chuang Tse said, "Nothing can be more beautiful than the simple."

Master Tie En Fang is oldest person of the fifth generation of Bagua in Beijing, and is my older brother in Bagua. He has studied Bagua with Master Liu Shi Kui since 1936. The government has a competition every year to find the oldest and healthiest people in China, and in 2004 Master Tie En Fang was one of the people honored. He is ninety-two years old. He still practices and teaches Bagua in the park every day. He walks three miles from his home to the park every day. We had a chance to talk a few years ago and, from his experience, he said the circle walk was the source of Bagua martial arts. He said it is the most important foundation exercise and that people should practice it every day for their whole lives. "I studied different forms from my teacher when I was young," Master Tie En Fang said, "but I always paid the most attention to the circle walk throughout my whole life." He recited a poem from Master Cheng Ting Hua, which could be translated into English like this:

> *Bagua martial arts are special martial arts, coming from heaven and the*
> *immortals.*
> *If you start learning Bagua from a young age, you are lucky*
> *Because you will have a chance to learn more.*
> *But the most important foundation exercise is the Bagua walk.*
> *Everybody should pay more attention to the walk, no matter if you are*
> *Young or old.*
> *Everybody should practice the Bagua walk throughout their whole lives.*
> *When you are getting older, you may forget the forms,*
> *But never forget the Bagua walk.*
> *If you keep up the practice of the Bagua walk, you can get*
> *Longevity, better health, and balance, and you can have a better life.*
> *In spiritual and physical body, you can get close to the immortals from the*
> *practice of the Bagua walk.*

Poetry by Cheng Ting Hua; calligraphy by Zhang Jie

Master Tie En Fang went on to say, "After I was fifty years old, I just focused my practice on the Bagua walk, single palm, and double palm. Right now I only focus on the Bagua walk. All my students over fifty years old have different health problems, stemming from the stress of the modern world. In the class I just teach them to practice the Bagua walk. Even if someone wants to learn more, I always say, 'No, focus on the Bagua walk, that is good enough for you.' If you want a long and happy life, focus on the Bagua walk. Right now, all of my students have good health and good, balanced emotions. I am ninety-two years old, I have a good appetite, good sleep, a good walk, I am able to take care of myself, and I also continue to help others by teaching Bagua. I've finished writing and publishing a book on Bagua. Everybody wants to become an immortal, but if I can live a good long life, feel good, and help others, that is the true life of an immortal. It is better than living forever. It is living well. The circle walk can help you to have this kind of life."

The origins of Bagua are rooted in the philosophy of the *I Ching*. The *I Ching* is literally a map of how change occurs in the universe, including nature, social relations, and humans. The *I Ching* states that although there are unlimited possibilities, they can be understood by the underlying processes that generate and develop these possibilities. The *I Ching* was developed to bridge the gap between the natural world and the world of reasoning and the mind.

The circle walk has two premises. One is that the movement of internal chi causes the external movement of the circle walk, once the chi has become strong and connected. Another premise is that within the master's mind there is already a very strong and clean understanding of the Bagua map, coming from the study of the *I Ching,* so when the external movement of circle walking happens, the master is able to understand and direct the movement in concert with the chi. The body is the car, the chi is the gas, and the mind is the understanding of how to drive and the directions to follow.

In the beginning, the circle walk was a natural movement. The master just listened to his body movement and walked in a circle. The old masters spent a great deal of time practicing every day, for generations, and they eventually began to understand that circle walking was the best way to achieve an internal, nonverbal understanding of the principles of the *I Ching.* They got great benefit from internal chi and being healthy, strong, and balanced. Walking the circle adds a depth of understanding to the principles of the *I Ching,* called "body reading" or "body knowledge." The masters began to develop and improve the circle walking practice generation after generation.

The circle walk is one of the best exercises to support health and achieve balance in your physical body, energy, and spirit. It is the best way to build a strong relationship and connection with nature, as well as between people in society. For these kinds of relationships Lao Tzu had an expression, "Tian Ren He Yi." This means that the individual person becomes one with nature in a spiritual fashion. Confucius had another word, "Ren Ai," which means that people should be connected together with a feeling of love. These two phrases are the most important goals of people's lives. Having a regular practice of the circle walk is one of the best ways to develop good and balanced chi, both internal and external.

I want to tell you a true story I heard from Master Xu Sheng Li (born 1939). His father was Master Xu Ming De (1899–1953), a great master of the fourth generation, who studied Bagua from Master Liu Bin. Master Xu Sheng Li told me that when he was a young boy, he went to Tian Tan Park with his father to practice Bagua. He met almost all of the masters of the fourth generation there, including Li Yan Chin, Liu Shi Kui, Wang Wen Kui, and others. The whole practice area was very quiet, for nobody was talking. When the masters arrived they just nodded to each other and then kept practicing. And everybody practiced the circle walk around a big pine tree. They walked very slowly, very balanced, with very good focus, relaxed and powerful. And you could see the circle they had made from walking around the tree.

Xu Sheng Li asked his father, "Why are they walking that way? They look like they are walking like a steam roller!" His father answered, "Yes, this is the Bagua circle walk. It is the most important foundation movement of Bagua Zhang. Remember to pay a lot of attention to this movement, and practice every day for your whole life. Walking more slowly, you receive more benefit." Shu asked, "Why?" His father answered, "No questions, just do it. In time your own practice will answer the question for you, just as I learned it from my own practice."

From this story and from my own experience, I understand the importance of practicing the circle walk as slowly as you can.

- Slow practice develops good balance. You don't want to move up and down or tip side to side as you walk, and going slowly helps you develop that skill.

- Slow walking helps you have better mental focus and develops your ability to concentrate. If you can concentrate well, you can deal with the stresses and challenges of life better, and they will affect your inner balance less.

- Slow walking helps your chi to sink down to your Dan Tian and stay there. Over time, the chi of your Dan Tian can grow stronger and more balanced, giving you real internal strength.

- Slow walking can help your whole body become more coordinated. It will make your legs very strong, balanced, and flexible, with an excellent ability to move. This is a very important foundation for health, longevity, and martial arts training.

All of these things together can open your body up to the universe. When your body is open to the universe, you naturally develop good health and let go of problems, whether they are physical, emotional, or mental. As your inside becomes clean and open, you are more and more connected to the energy of the universe and can absorb the "nutrition" that it brings. This means that you have better harmony with the universe. Just like Lao Tzu said, "The highest stage of life is Tian Ren He Yi," when nature and person become as one.

Standing Chi Gong Preparation for the Circle Walk

- While standing in the Chian Gua, or the northwest corner trigram, face to the south. Your whole body is relaxed and you should focus your awareness on your Dan Tian. Adjust your breathing so it is long, slow, and even, with the tip of your tongue gently touching the roof of the mouth. (See photos, page 66.)

- Then, start lifting both arms up from your sides, palms down. Focus your attention on gathering the Yin chi from the earth at the Lao Gung point on your palm. The Lao Gung point is located on the middle of your palm. As you raise your arms, breathe in gently to assist in drawing the Yin chi to the hand (1).

- Extend your left arm, your eyes looking to your left palm, and then extend the right arm, looking to the right. Gently exhale as you do this (2 and 3).

- Continue extending and raising both arms up to the sky, taking the Yang chi in from the sky and also from the Lao Gung point. Breathe in gently (4).

- Relax your whole body, especially the arms, and let the arms drop down just slightly. Breathe out gently.

- Twist your body to the left, with your hands still above your head, taking in the Yang chi from nature to the Lao Gung point. Gently breathe in (5).

- Let the body untwist naturally until your eyes are facing forward again, as you gently breathe out (6).

- Twist your body to the right side, with your hands still above your head, taking in the Yin chi from nature to the Lao Gung point, as you gently breathe in (7).

- Let the body untwist naturally, until your eyes are facing forward, as you gently breathe out (8).

- Push both palms up to the sky, extending your arms, and concentrate on letting the Yin and Yang chi mix together in the palms. Gently inhale and keep looking forward (9).

- Drop down both hands while drawing them to the left (10), then right (11), then down in front of your body (12), with your eyes following your hands. End with your hands pressing down below your Dan Tian, palms down. Breathe out gently. The Yin chi and the Yang chi follow your hands and go down through the Bai Hui point, down the central channel, and to the Dan Tian. Let it stay there. Your body is slightly sitting down, with bent knees.

Standing Chi Gong Preparation

Beginning stance

1

2

3

4

5

6

7

8

9

10

11

12

Keep these additional thoughts in mind while doing the movements:

- With all of the movements, you should grasp the ground gently with your toes, and your tongue should keep touching the roof of your mouth.

- During all of the movements, the top of your head is always pressing up to the sky. Draw back your chin slightly, so that all five points—your Bai Hui point, upper Dan Tian, middle Dan Tian, lower Dan Tian (which is also referred to as just "Dan Tian"), and Hui Yin point—are aligned with the central channel.

- When you finish your hand movement, your hands have described the Bagua circle and the change of Yin and Yang.

- At this time, you should be feeling that you're making a chi sphere or "bowl" around your body. At first, picture a chi sphere around you. Later you will feel it and you won't need the picture. Your body always stays in the center of this sphere as you practice. You should always keep aware of the chi sphere, but you will forget and lose the feeling. You should keep going back, noticing the feeling and remembering the picture, until eventually you will be able to feel it strongly and have it stay with you whenever you practice.

Feeling the sphere has three functions. First, your body and spirit can continue to take in good energy from the universe and remove the bad chi or disease from your body through the sphere. The sphere is an open system, a bridge between the individual and the universe. Second, the sphere is a bridge between you and other people. When people come near you, they must come within your sphere before they can physically touch you, and by having a strong sense of your chi sphere, you will be much more aware of what is around you so you can more readily react. Third, the sphere can make your spirit and physical body much more balanced and stable. Like a baby being held by its mother, our bodies are nurtured and supported by the chi sphere. When you practice Bagua, you should have the feeling of always being aware of the chi sphere, no matter if you are practicing the single palm, eight mother palms, weapons, or any other exercise.

It is important to remember that everyone living has this sphere, but they don't notice it, so they can't interact with it. But Bagua training can help you to take back this talent that people have forgotten or lost due to the stress of life. Compared to people, animals are much more in tune with this primary talent. For example, during the December 2004 tsunami in South Asia, people couldn't find any dead animals in the aftermath because they all ran away before the tsunami came. One person had a group of elephants that he had trained to give tourists rides on the beach. Before the tsunami came, all of the elephants stopped working. Usually they were very gentle and well mannered, but that day they weren't. They were very agitated, although no one yet knew why. The master of the elephants tried to quiet them and get them back to work, but he couldn't. This was very unusual. Some of the elephants that were held in leg chains so they couldn't get away broke out of their chains and wanted to leave. The master began to understand that something strange and bad was happening. He just let the elephants leave. As the elephants were leaving, they grabbed some of the tourists with their trunks and put them on their backs as they ran up to the hills. The elephants were not only able to save their own lives, but the lives of their master and some of the lucky tourists.

Scientists say that elephants can hear sounds much better than humans, and they may have been able to hear the subtle sounds of the tsunami coming over the water. Humans used to have the ability to hear and feel these types of things, but we have lost this ability. But the circle walk and the best chi gong exercises can help people regain this innate talent. Being able to feel your chi sphere is a big step toward finding out about your inner nature.

During the standing chi gong movements, your physical body and spirit start to feel more connected, and you also feel the connection between yourself and nature. This is an example of Tien Ren He Yi. And when your feelings are much more connected to your spirit, it is called Xing Ming Shuang Xiu. (See page 3.) Xing is Yin and Ming is Yang. The goal of Xing Ming Shuang Xiu is to make a new balance between your spirit and physical body.

Starting the Circle Walk

- Keep both palms keep pressing down, fingers facing fingers, with Tiger Mouth open. This is called Shuang Ta Zhang (1). (See photos, page 72.)

- Drop down both shoulders and elbows, along with the palms. This is called Chen Jian Zhui Zhou.

- Lift the top of your head to the sky, helping the neck to be straight. Draw back the chin a little bit. This is called Xuan Ding Shu Xang.

- Your upper back is a little curved and expanding. The chest is curved slightly inward. This is called Xi Xiong Jen Bei.

- The lower back is relaxed, the buttocks drop down and forward, and the tailbone goes gently forward and down a little bit. This is called Ta Yao Liu Tun. The function of this position is to help you open up and have more feeling in the Dan Tian. Also, it can make the chi circulate more smoothly in the back and legs.

- A beginner or someone with weak knees should bend the knees just a bit. As your legs become more balanced, relaxed, and strong, you can bend your knees more, but it is important not to hurt your knees, so don't overdo it. This is called Chu Xi. There are three levels or "basins"—upper, middle, and lower—depending on how much you bend your knees. Most new students should keep to the upper level, in which your knees are only bent a little, maybe fifteen to thirty degrees. After three years of practice, students are often ready to try the middle level of walking, in which the knees are bent thirty to sixty degrees. In the lower level the knees are very bent, from sixty to ninety degrees or even slightly more. To do this you should have over ten years of experience and have excellent leg strength and flexibility. The different levels have different kinds of benefits in strengthening your legs and balance. Of course, you gain more benefits if you can do the lower stance, but you also risk hurting yourself. My experience is that the upper level is good enough for your health and longevity. However, as Confucius says, everything should be done in moderation. Doing too much causes trouble, while doing too little won't work very well.

- Squeeze together your legs, thighs, and knees. This is called scissor legs, or Jianzi Tui.

- Start the walk from the inside foot, and move the foot straight forward (2). When you step with the outside foot, it moves in an arc. When the inside foot moves forward, it passes very close to the outside foot as you gently touch the legs and ankles together. When the outside foot moves it doesn't come in so close but follows the arc of the circle (3). This part of the stepping is called Me Ging or ankles touching.

The entire technique is called Li Zhi Wai Kou. The inside foot goes straight; the outside foot goes in a curve. The function of this is to keep the knees and the thighs connected and squeezed together. This gives better balance and stability while walking. Also, this has the effect of strengthening the reproductive system. The Chinese chi gong exercises, and especially the Taoist chi gong exercises, pay a lot of attention to strengthening the reproductive system. Usually the meditation masters would be encouraged to abstain from sex, but they recognized that keeping sexual energy balanced and strong is important for health and vitality. The circle walk is good for this. Also, if you have good sexual energy, you have good health and good feelings in your body and spirit. Good health and good feelings encourage good relationships with your family and community. In turn, a balanced family and community encourage good relationships between families and communities, and even throughout the whole city and country.

Basic Circle Walk

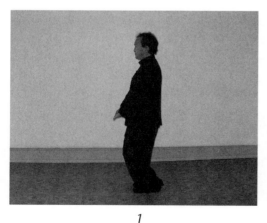

1

2

3

Changing Direction During the Circle Walk

You start walking around the circle by going counterclockwise from the northwest corner of the circle, called the Chian Gua. This is the Yin direction of walking. You may walk around once, three times, or as many times you like. Then you can change to walking in the clockwise direction, called the Yang direction. You should walk the same number of times around the circle both ways, to make the Yin and Yang balanced. However, the change should take place at the northwest corner, where you started the walk.

- Changing direction starts with the outside foot, in this case the right foot. (See photos, page 74.) The right foot turns in to make a T formation with the left foot, with the knees and thighs squeezing together. Have seventy percent of your weight on the back leg and thirty percent on the front. Your face and upper body stay facing forward. This is called Ko Bu (1). Also, please remember that Ko Bu should be small, to emphasize the closing and squeezing of the lower body (especially the reproductive system). The function of Ko Bu is to start twisting the body, which helps to open up the groin, the hips, the kua, and the Dan Tian.

- Move the weight of the body to the right foot. Turn your upper body back 180 degrees, with the left foot stepping down on the circle, pointing to where you came from. The feet should be toed out to ninety degrees or a little bit more, with seventy percent of the weight on the right foot, and thirty percent on the left foot. Open your hips and kua as much as you can, with your eyes looking back to where you came from. The heel of the left foot should line up with the heel of the right foot. This is called Bai Bu (2). Right now your whole hip and groin area should be open and relaxed. The combination of the Ko Bu step and the Bai Bu step strengthens your ability to open and close the legs and hips, to squeeze and release.

- After the Bai Bu step, start walking in the Yang direction (clockwise), beginning with the right foot. Everything is the same walking in the other direction, except the right foot is now the inside foot, and the left foot is now the outside foot (3, 4).

Changing Direction During the Circle Walk Photos

1

2

3　　　　　　　　　　　　　4

The Function of Ko Bu and Bai Bu

Ko Bu and Bai Bu have many benefits. First, this practice strengthens the muscles of the back and legs, because strong legs and walking are a very important foundation for health. When people are getting older or sick, the first thing that happens is the legs get weak. So stronger legs and good skill at walking can greatly benefit your health.

Second, Ko Bu and Bai Bu improve the circulation of the chi and blood. The energy meridians of the legs are exercised and developed by this squeeze-and-relax cycle.

Third, this practice strengthens the internal organs so they can work better, and makes more chi and blood to benefit the body.

Fourth, it strengthens the reproductive system and sexual energy to support health.

Fifth, it gives the body good balance, both at rest and in motion.

And finally, the biggest part of this Ko Bu-Bai Bu stepping pattern is to develop the change between Yin and Yang within the body.

The Change Between the Yin and Yang of the Body During the Circle Walk

When you are walking the circle, the inside foot is Yin and the outside foot is Yang. The back foot is Yin and the front foot is Yang. For example, when you are walking in the Yin direction, you should start from the left foot, and the left foot is Yin. When you start to walk, the left foot starts the change from Yin to Yang. When you finish the step, the left foot is still Yin, but it is in front, which means that it is half Yin and half Yang. Also, at the same time, the right foot was Yang, but then it becomes more Yin as it becomes the back foot. When the left foot finishes the step forward, the Yin and the Yang on both feet are balanced. Also, as you continue to walk, the right foot moves forward and changes to full or true Yang. This is because the right foot is in the Yang position both from the direction of the walk and the relationship of the legs. The function of the change between the Yin and Yang of the feet is to adjust the Yin and the Yang of the whole body so they can be balanced. Good and balanced Yin and Yang means the student will enjoy more health and better circulation of the chi and blood.

When you change direction, the Yin and the Yang of the feet start to change as well. For example, the right foot changes from Yang to Yin, from outside to inside. The left foot changes from inside to outside, from Yin to Yang. As you practice over time, this starts to develop the natural chi circulation, as well as the muscles, tendons, joints, the mind, and the nervous system. For example, when walking in the Yang direction, you use certain muscles more, and the coordination of the body is all oriented one way, so walking the circle both ways balances this out. One side of the brain controls one side of the body, and so by walking one way you are emphasizing one side more. By walking the circle equally both ways, you develop each side the same, so your body can learn to become more balanced and coordinated. When people get sick, are in a bad mood, or are feeling tired and exhausted, their minds are unbalanced. One part of the mind is overactive, while other parts are inactive. Over time, when the mind is unbalanced, the problems of emotions, thoughts, and the physical body will get worse. The body and mind are connected, but the mind controls the body. By practicing in a balanced way, the body and mind can learn to return to balance. Over time the body can heal itself and develop, and so can the emotions and the mind. They all work together in harmony.

Ding Shi, or Single Standing Meditation

After you practice the basic circle walk with palms pressing down, over time your body will start to change and develop the proper feeling of Bagua. From the natural body you develop into a Bagua body. Usually you need to practice the circle walk for three years until the body develops properly. Then you can begin practicing the single standing posture, or standing meditation, which comes from the Bagua walk. A student will usually do the single standing posture practices for another three years.

For example, while walking around a tree, you step with left Ko Bu, and your toes point toward the tree. Then you take a big right Bai Bu step, with your right heel facing to the tree. You open up the hips, thighs, and groin. The angle of your knee joint is ninety degrees, as if you are sitting down. Both palms continue to push down, at the same level as your knees. At the same time, your eyes look back over your right shoulder. Your whole body is twisting. The top of your head keeps lifting up. Then you hold the posture for as long as you can.

Over time, this practice can give you a good foundation to practice more advanced movements. What do I mean by a good foundation? It means that your body is more open, your muscles are stronger, you have much better balance, a much stronger root, a strong feeling of internal chi and spirit, and good concentration. The circle walk is more Yang and Dong (moving), and the single standing posture is Yin and Jing (still). In other words, the circle walk is strong and moving and the single standing posture is soft and still. The two practices complement each other.

Heng Kai Zhang, or Single Palm Change

Heng Kai Zhang, or the single palm change, is the first movement on the way from Bagua chi gong to martial arts. Practicing it continues to open your body and mind to the universe, opens up your meridians, and strengthens your chi and blood to support health. The single palm change helps to build harmony between you and the universe, and between the

Yin and Yang of your body. It also strengthens and tones the muscles, extends and tones the ligaments, and strengthens the root of your body, giving you good balance. During the practice of single palm, your body starts to get used to changing directions with great balance; when you need to protect yourself, you want to be able to move and change quickly and smoothly. Also, the single palm change includes many foundation techniques of application. Learning it can help you start understanding the applications of Bagua as well as the foundations of Chinese philosophy.

The single palm is a special tool for studying and understanding Chinese philosophy. I talked before about the philosophy of the Bagua walk, and I said that walking on the Bagua map was a technique of genius, a pioneering step forward in both chi gong and martial arts. First, Bagua is special in its circularity. Everything in the universe has a circular nature, and so does any individual thing. People have their "sphere of influence," and the earth is a sphere that orbits in a circle, as does the sun. No matter if it is the sun, the earth, or the cells in our body, everything moves in circles, and the cycle of life and death is also circular. When you are walking on the Bagua circle, it is a model of the individual traveling within the universe, in an orbit.

Second, the Bagua masters considered any individual human being to be a part of the universe. You can't be in the world without being a part of it.

Third, the old masters of Bagua, when they developed the walking methods that we now practice, had the goal of developing in the individual a conscious awareness of his connection with the universe, to achieve an understanding of the nature of reality that is beyond words. In Chinese philosophy there is an expression for this: "Tian Ren He Yi." This means developing a high level of harmony between man and the universe.

How does the single palm fit in with this? First, with the single palm movement, the Bagua masters tried to make a Bagua map with your body. Compared to the Bagua walk, this is an important development. We already talked about the Bagua map being a model of the universe. By walking on the circle, you step out the pattern with your walking. But in the single palm change, the movement of your whole body is making the "shape" of the Bagua map. The circle walk shows that people are in the world, while the single palm change shows that the world is within our bodies as well. Or we could say that the Bagua masters show people a model of the universe through special body language.

The second point is that the circle walk shows that the universe and people should be as one, to create the best harmony. The single palm shows that human beings are the "owners" of the relationship between people and the universe. By this we mean that people have to choose and develop that connection, as they also can avoid it and stay disconnected. Humans have the initiative; they have the choice. The universe has given us the opportunity, but it is our own actions that can help or hinder harmony. The function of single palm—its health, development, and philosophy—comes from the circle walk. The martial arts elements, on the other hand, come from the treasures of traditional martial arts, such as wrestling. You can see how traditional Chinese philosophy, health, vitality, and martial arts are all related together, are all wonderfully integrated into one. The single palm change is the root of this connection.

Single Palm Change: Yan Kou Huan Shi

All of the principles of the circle walk should be used when practicing the single palm change. But since the single palm has some things different from the basic walk, you need to know how to change from the circle walk to single palm. This is called Yan Kou Huan Shi.

- Begin by walking on the circle in the Yin direction (counterclockwise), in the circle walk form. (See photos, page 81.)

- Make a small Ko Bu with the outside foot, in this case the right foot. The knees and thighs are close together and gently squeezed (1).

- Your body turns back 180 degrees into Bai Bu, looking in the new direction. At the same time, the left arm protects your back, bending at the elbow about thirty degrees, with the palm sideways facing out. The right palm pushes down behind the right ribs and hip. Seventy percent of the weight is on the back or right leg. Between both arms and palms, there is the feeling of extending away from the body. The right arm is Ta (extending and pressing down) and the left arm is Choung (extending and pressing out). The hips are open (2).

- The body twists back a little bit, to make a small circle with the right palm. Then the right palm turns up, close to the right rib (3). Then the body moves forward and turns about 180 degrees, pivoting around the left leg. The right foot moves forward with the body, stepping into Gou Gua Bu (hooking foot step). The right palm moves around your body, from the right rib, around the chest, to the left ribs, and then stretches out so the palm is under the left armpit. Your eyes follow your body's turn and you finish by looking in the direction the right palm is pointing (pretty much behind you). At the same time, the left hand continues to push forward with Choung Jin (extending action) and protects the right shoulder. Seventy percent of the weight of the body is on the left leg, and you are standing in a Ko Bu stance. This movement is called Ye Di Cang Hua, or Flower Hidden Under the Leaves (4).

- Your body turns in to the center of the circle. At the same time you extend both arms away from your body and both palms turn up. The left palm is a bit behind the right palm. Your eyes look to the right palm and your feet don't move. Your toes grasp the ground, making a strong root. This is called Gu Yan Chu Chun, or Single Goose Leaves the Flock. The same movement is also called Heng Kai Zhang, or horizontal palm change (5).

- Your body continues to turn to the center of the circle. Both arms continue to move toward the center of the circle along with the body. Your right palm changes into Li Zhang, also known as Tiger Mouth or standing palm. Your body turns in to the center of the circle. Your fingers point up to the sky and the left palm is positioned under the right elbow, with the left middle finger three inches away from the elbow. This is called Huai Bao Dan Yu (Holding Single Fish); Huai Bao Chi Xing (Holding the Seven Stars); or Huai Bao Yin Yang (Holding the Yin and Yang) (6).

- At this point, the right palm is Yang and the left palm is Yin. The right palm pushes forward while the body stays back. Your chest is a little bit in, so the hand and chest have the feeling of being apart. This is called Cheng, or extending. At the same time, the left palm pushes in and the arms squeeze a little bit together. This is called Guo. Both arms working together are called Choung Guo Li. The function of Choung Guo Li is to make the whole body much more stable and coordinated. Your eyes look to the center of the circle, through the right Tiger Mouth.

- The top of your head stays lifted as you gently draw back your chin and stretch your neck. Shoulders and elbows are relaxed and down. The lower body is relaxed, your bottom moves forward and down a bit, and the whole body sinking down. Both legs are crossed, like Jian Zi Twei (scissor legs). This is called single palm, and all of the combined techniques together can be called Yan Kou Huan Shi. For the single palm walk, keep the position of your upper body and begin to walk around the circle from the inside foot, in this case the right foot. The walking is the same as the basic circle walk.

Yan Kou Huan Shi Photos

Beginning stance

1

2

3

4

5

6

The Tiger Mouth Palm

The Tiger Mouth Palm is the most frequently used palm in Liu Shi Bagua. When you learn and practice single palm change, you pay particular attention to making the palm just right. In single palm, the fingers of the palm point upward, with the thumb pointing horizontally to the side. One by one, each of the four fingers twist inward to make the center of the palm slightly curved. At the same time, the fingers are extended strongly, and the finger and thumb tips just barely flex, as if you were trying to palm a basketball. Walking with Tiger Mouth, you would look out and see the imaginary center of the Bagua circle in the left window between your thumb and index finger. Emphasizing the Tiger Mouth in practice brings good awareness to the hand. When practicing single palm change, focus on both good hand position and good waist movement, and you can develop good awareness in the Dan Tian area, which also helps to concentrate chi in the Dan Tian. Good posture of hand, good posture of mind, good concentration of chi.

How to Change Direction with the Single Palm Walk

- Your outside foot, in this case the left foot, turns in again into a small Ko Bu, with seventy percent of the weight on the back foot. (See photos, page 84.) At the same time, twist your right palm to be in front of your chest with the elbow more bent. Both arms and palms are expanding, while your eyes look forward in the direction of the inside foot. This is called Ko Bu He Zhang, or Ko Bu with closing palm (1).

- Your body turns back 180 degrees with Bai Bu. Both arms and palms keep the same position, moving with the body. This is called Zhuan Shen Bai Bu, or Turning Body with Bai Bu (2).

- Your left foot moves forward into Ko Bu with Gou Gua, or hooking step. At the same time, the left palm stretches back under the right armpit, while the right palm keeps pushing forward to protect the left shoulder with Choung Jin. Your eyes look back to the left palm. Seventy percent of the weight is on the back leg, which is the right leg in this example. This is called Ye Di Cang Hua (3).

- Left Gu Yan Chu Chen (Single Goose Leaves Flock). This is the same as before, just with the opposite arms (4).

- Left Hai Bao Dan Yu (Holding Single Fish). Same as before (5).

- Start walking from the inside foot, in this case the left foot. Walk in the Yin direction again.

Changing Direction with Single Palm Walk Photos

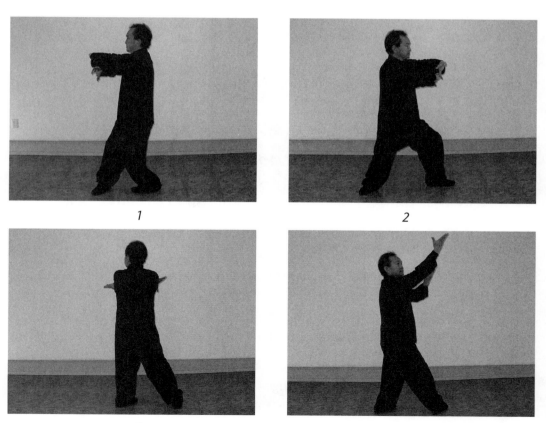

1

2

3

4

5

Running Horse, or Zou Ma Huo Xie

Zou Ma Huo Xie is another distinguishing movement of Nan Cheng Bagua Zhang. This movement comes from the Ye Di Cang Hua of the single palm change. In practice, it is most often used right after Turning Back Palm, or Pu Tui You Shen (see below), but it can also be done within the single palm change and is traditionally taught first.

Compared to the single palm change, Zou Ma Huo Xie is more difficult to perform, but it also gives greater benefits, both for applications and the health and vitality of the practitioner.

This is how to practice Zou Ma Huo Xie:

- Beginning after movement two of the single palm change, or Zhuan Bai Bu, you move your weight from your left leg to your right leg, into big Si Liu Bu. (See photos, page 86.) At the same time, start to bring your right arm back a bit toward your right side, keeping the same arm posture (1).

- Your body and waist make a big right turn as you look back over your right shoulder. Your left arm stays bent and pushes forward, moving with the body but not crossing the centerline.

- At the same time, your right arm makes a circle on the right side of the body, as you twist the whole arm with shoulder relaxed, with the right palm twisting and turning up. The right hand ends up next to the ribs, just touching. Your eyes follow the right palm (2).

- Your body turns back to the left side, into Ye Di Cang Hua. Your right foot steps forward with Gou Gua Bu, or hooking foot, into Bu Ding Bu Ba Zhi Bu, or small Ko Bu. The whole body is very coiled. Your eyes still look to the right palm. This is the same as the single palm change (3).

- Heng Kai Zhang, or horizontal palm, and Gu Yan Chu Chun, or Single Goose Leaves the Flock. Again, this is the same as the single palm change (4).

- Huai Bao Dan Yu, or Holding Single Fish. Again, like single palm (5).

- Walk the other way.

Running Horse Photos

1   2

3

4

5

Turning Back Palm: Pu Tui You Shen

Pu Tui You Shen is another model movement of Beijing Nan Cheng Bagua and is distinct to this Bagua school. Why is Pu Tui You Shen important?

Pu Tui You Shen has the same health benefits as practicing the circle walk and single palm change, but the applications are different. You Shen is extremely useful when you are being controlled with an arm lock. You Shen allows you to "turn the tables" on your opponent by "unlocking" the lock and moving toward your opponent to counter. During the movement of You Shen, your whole body should be twisting and moving forward. In Nan Cheng Bagua, we call this Gun Zhe Jing. This means twisting your body and moving close to the person, to his side or behind him. The waist is the center of the movement, which is similar to the circle walk and single palm change, when the core of the body is also the waist. In addition, You Shen enables you to move directly backwards. It also strengthens the legs and the squatting action of the hips.

The You Shen movement is a part of every form. It is extremely important for applications and for developing a good foundation. The third palm of eight mother palms is called Bei Shen Zhang. The You Shen movement is the root of the third mother palm, but the Bei Shen Zhang is more difficult.

Here's how you practice You Shen:

- You first start out in the single palm walk on the Bagua circle, walking in the Yin direction (counterclockwise), with your left palm extending to the center and your left foot forward. (See photos, page 89.)

- Ko Bu He Zhang. Same as single palm (1).

- Pu Tui. Your body turns left, you extend the left leg back, and you bend the right knee. Your weight is on the right leg, almost sitting down. Your right palm pushes back with fingers pointing down, arm fully extended. Your left shoulder, arm, and palm are all twisting and extending. You move your hand behind the left hip with your palm facing up, your fingers twisting and following the line of the leg (2).

- Your body weight moves from the right leg to the left leg into left Gung Bu. At the same time, the right palm keeps pushing back, and the left shoulder, arm, and palm keep twisting, extending, and moving forward, ending at shoulder height. Your eyes look forward to the left palm (3).

- The left palm moves up in Liao Zhang, with the pinkie on the top. Your arm keeps twisting and extending. Usually from here you would move into Running Horse.

Pu Tui You Shen Photos

1

2

3

Single Palm Extensions

The single palm change is a fundamental movement of Bagua Zhang. The basic concept is changing directions from the single palm posture. However, there are many variations or extensions of the movement. These use the same basic motions as the single palm change, but continue and extend them. They are important for body flexibility and for martial applications.

Single Palm with Water Lily

Everything is like single palm until you turn your palm over.

- Arms extend with palms up, your body turning into the circle (1).

- The right Yang palm continues to twist, making a horizontal circle in front of your face. At the same time, your body makes a small twisting circle from the waist. The movement comes from the waist and goes out to the hand. Then, push forward to the center of the circle. At the same time, the left Yin palm turns down to protect your right ribcage, really extending around (2).

- When you finish, both palms make the "holding the fish" position with Cheng Guo Li (3).

Water Lily Photos

1

2

3

Single Palm with Cloud Hand

Cloud Hand could be explained as a bigger version of Water Lily Palm.

- Same as Water Lily (1).

- The right Yang palm continues to make a big horizontal circle around your head. At the same time, your waist makes a small circle. Your eyes follow and look at the Yang palm (2).

- Finish the circle with your right arm, ending with the palm facing center, like Holding Single Fish. At the same time, your left Yin palm protects your right ribcage and pushes harder. This helps to make the body more stable. This is Yin and Yang in balance (3).

Cloud Hand Photos

1

2

3

Single Palm with Tuo Tian Zhang, Lifting Palms to Heaven

This one has two variations, with a single or double Bai-Ko step. This is the single version, also called Dan Bai Dan Ko. The Shuang Bai Shuang Ko step will be detailed in the Twenty-Four Movements of Five Elements, Three Levels form, in the second book we are working on.

- Begin from Ye Di Cang Hua (1).

- Standing with Si Liu Bu, both palms push up to heaven, to one side. The right Yang palm is overhead, and the left Yin palm is under the right elbow with your body sinking down (2).

- Your right leg steps into Ko Bu, stepping around the left foot. At the same time, the right palm protects the left ribs under the left armpit. The left palm continues to rise up to the heavens. Your body faces outside the circle (3).

- Your left foot makes a step into Shun Bu. Your body turns to the Yin direction of the circle. The left palm makes a Water Lily Palm motion, ending in a single palm change with Single Fish and Cheng Guo Li (4).

Lifting Palms to Heaven Photos

1

2

3

4

Single Palm with Five Step Cloud Palm Change

- Your inside foot, the left foot, steps into Bai Bu (1).

- Your left foot steps into Ko Bu (2).

- Left Bai Bu (3).

- Right Ko Bu (4).

- Left Shun Bu, making one small circle (5).

Five Step Cloud Palm Change Photos

1

2

3

4

5

Single Palm with Shuang Bai Shuang Ko Bu

As you make these steps, your arms do the same basic motions of the Cloud Hand Palm, adjusting for the different timing of the steps. It is important to notice the similarities and differences between the Five Step Cloud Palm and the Shuang Bai Shuang Ko Bu step from the Five Elements Form. (The Five Elements Form will be detailed in the second book.) The Cloud Palm uses small Bai/Ko steps; you take five steps to make one circle. In Shuang Bai Shuang Ko Bu, you take five steps to make two smaller circles. (See photos, below.) So it uses big Bai/Ko steps—you have to make much larger Bai and Ko steps to get the two circles in.

Shuang Bai Shuang Ko Bu Photos

1

2

3

4

5

Single Palm Change Using Bai Kou Huan Shi

There is another method of single palm change called Bai Kou Huan Shi. The difference is that Bai Kou Huan Shi begins with the inside foot. The inside foot makes a twisting Bai Bu step, as you put your weight on the back leg and turn your head to look back over the inside shoulder. Then the outside foot does the Ko Bu, while the body starts to turn to look back, with Ta Zhang (pressing down) and Zhuang Zhang (extending and pressing out). Then the new outside foot steps out in Shun Bu, or natural step. The final step is the same—make a hook foot and finish the motion as in Yan Kou Huan Shi.

Why is this variation important? I think that there are at least two reasons. Since an attack can happen at any time, you can't just say, "Not yet, I'm on the wrong foot." In that case, you will get punched. If you are on the outside foot when you need to change, you can start the change with your inside foot. Another reason is that when you practice both variations and can use both, your body and spirit will be more complete, as the two movements complement each other. Otherwise, your body, energy, and spirit can become unbalanced. I learned about Bai Kou Huan Shi from my Bagua brother Master Xu Sheng Li, who studied under his father, Master Xu Ming De. And Master Xu Ming De studied under Liu Bin. But most masters only use Yan Kou Huan Shi, and if Master Xu Sheng Li had not taught this to me, it would have perhaps been lost forever. I am very grateful to Master Xu Sheng Li for passing this on.

Bai Kou Huan Shi Photos

1

2

3

4

5

Bai Ko Single Palm Change Photos

Yin and Yang Arm Spirals

This exercise strengthens the root of your body, particularly the legs. It makes your body more stable. It also strengthens the core of the body, the waist and hips area. Another benefit of this exercise is to loosen up and strengthen your shoulder and arms. Overall, this exercise prepares you to practice the regular exercises and applications with spiral power. Done lightly, it is a good warm-up exercise.

Yang Arm Spirals

Begin by standing in a fifty-fifty stance (Horse Stance), facing to the south. The legs are about shoulder width apart and parallel. The legs are also relaxed and basically straight. The left hand touches your waist with the Tiger Mouth area of your palm. The right hand starts at the right waist, palm up and fingers pointing forward. Then turn your waist to the left as you extend your fingers toward the left and away from your body. When your hand reaches shoulder level, swing the palm out to the right side, with the arm extended and the palm up. Once it reaches your side, twist the arm and palm, so the palm goes behind your head, and around until it is above your left ear, and then finish the overhead circle. Then continue to swing your arm around in front of your head and back to the right side of your body, with the palm turning down. Then bring your palm back up and underneath your armpit. This is the same as the beginning posture. From there, lift your palm and make a tight circle near your right shoulder, keeping the palm up. Then turn the palm down in front of your body and then back around to the side, palm facing back. Then bring your palm up so the fingers are facing the ribs and the palm facing the armpit. These are the Yang spirals, one big one overhead and one little one above your shoulder. Repeat eight times, and then switch to using the other arm.

Yang Arm Spirals Photos

1

2

3

4

5

6

7

8

9

10

Yin Arm Spirals

Everything is the same for this exercise, except the arm goes backwards. Instead of moving the arm in a pushing or Yang way, you move the arm by pulling it from the waist and shoulders. The positions are the same; just reverse the order.

Whether you are doing this in the Yang or Yin direction, you should pay attention to moving with the waist and the whole body. Also, in this exercise, it is okay to lean, turn, and shift a bit as you do it. You don't have to be totally upright the whole time. Sometimes your body wants to twist a little off axis, and for this exercise that is OK. Finally, don't forget to practice using each hand equally each way. As you practice this exercise over time, you should vary the order in which you practice it, and eventually you can progress to using both arms at the same time. Since this exercise is very simple, it is a good one for practicing all the possibilities and all the variations.

Continued Bai Bu and Ko Bu Step with Hooking Foot

This basic exercise is a part of the Bagua stepping. There are two main functions. The first is to strengthen your legs, which will give you much more balance with single leg standing. The second is to teach you how to remove your leg when someone tries to control your foot or leg. You just pick up the leg and use the circle to get out of the way. Also, it teaches you how to control another person's leg and body using a hooking foot.

Begin in a natural standing position. Your hands can be held behind your back or at your waist, whichever is most comfortable.

Lift your right knee, toes pointed down. Circle your foot to the left side and in front of your leg, then forward, then out to the right side, and return it to in front of your body. From here, step down in front with a twisting Bai Bu. At the same time as you step, bend your left leg, with your whole body sinking down as the top of your head goes up. For the leg spirals, it is important to keep your upper body just like you were doing the circle walk. To make a continued Ko Bu step simply reverse the order, and then step down into a Ko Bu step.

Hooking Foot Photos

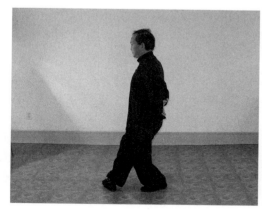

1
                                    2

3   4

Martial Applications of Heng Kai Zhang

Heng Kai Zhang came from techniques of Chinese traditional wrestling, called Bie Tze, which includes Shou Bie Tze and Jiao Bie Tze. Bie Tze means twisting throw. Shou Bie Tze uses the arms to throw, while Jiao Bie Tze uses the legs and arms to throw. But the single palm movement has both, and it is more elegant and efficient.

To gain a basic understanding of these principles, please study these application pictures. (See photos below.) All of these techniques use power from the waist, which is developed through the motion of Heng Kai Zhang. They also use coordinated power from the spine and waist to the tip of the finger. The Nan Cheng Bagua term for waist movement is Zou Yao. The term for coordinated body power is Shao Li. When using these applications, the power always moves along the circle, either a horizontal circle or a vertical circle. Please remember—Zou Yao power comes from the waist, and Shao Li uses coordinated power like a whip.

Martial Applications Photos

1 (a)

1 (b)

2 (a)

2 (b)

2 (c)

3 (a)

3 (b)

3 (c)

4 (a)

4 (b)

5 (a)

5 (b)

6 (a)

6 (b)

6 (c)

7 (a)

7 (b)

8 (a)

8 (b)

8 (c)

Chapter Four

Sixteen Zhan Zhuang Exercises

As I've described previously, the martial arts movements and techniques are only a part of the Bagua system—the younger and shallower part, which is easiest to see and describe. The essence of the Bagua palm system is the special chi gong exercises, or internal energy development exercises. Their function is to help you develop and understand internal chi, and to give you a better foundation to continue practicing the Bagua palm.

There are two main types of chi exercises. Zou Zhuang refers to the circle walk and single palm walking, which includes all the circle walking practices with the various arm and body motions. The second kind of chi exercise is Zhan Zhuang, which means standing chi exercise. The meaning of Zhuang is "the big roots and strong trunk of a big tree." Doing these exercises builds and develops your "body tree," making your body strong, supple, and connected to the earth and nature. The standing practice can be done by itself, or it can be done before practicing circle walk exercises. Bagua emphasizes the Zou Zhuang type of exercise, while the standing exercises are used to develop the balance, awareness, and power that are used in walking. However, the serious student keeps going back to the standing practices.

If you look at the walking practice as Yang, the standing practices are more Yin. But you should understand and remember that everything is made of both Yin and Yang. In Yang there is always the seed of Yin, and the Yin has the seed of Yang within it as well. The seed of Yin can grow or the seed of the Yang can grow. As you develop the Yin or Yang, the relationship between them can develop and complement each other, and eventually the essence of the thing or person itself can change.

When you practice the standing exercise, it has two major benefits. First, it strengthens your internal chi, and second, it develops the principles of martial power and technique. Here are the principles of the standing form:

- Pay attention to the preparation part of the form. In the preparation part, you use belly breathing. The whole body is naturally relaxed. Intention is focused on your Dan Tian. But when you use the belly breathing you must remember not to do it too hard. The breath needs to be natural and soft. This is very important. All of the movements must be made with the feeling of more expansion and more extension. Practiced over time, this makes the bowl or sphere of chi larger, stronger, and more balanced. In Chinese, this feeling is called Hun Yuan or feeling the bowl of energy. Your body and spirit are kept in the middle of the bowl. The bowl is made of your chi, and your body and mind, even your spirit, are important parts of generating this Hum Yuan. Once you find and develop this feeling in the standing exercises, all the exercises should have this feeling.

- If you can do very well with the first two principles, which take time to do, you will start to have stronger internal chi in your Dan Tian. This type of chi is called chen chi or true chi. Everyone has the seed of chi or natural chi. As you grow up, you use this energy to do things—eating, working, exercising, thinking, or whatever else you do. If you live a balanced lifestyle, this chi can stay strong and good, but if your life is out of balance, this chi is depleted. But if you practice the standing exercises and all of the Bagua exercises, you begin to develop the nice, natural chi that can make you stronger. You begin to change the essence of chi to chen chi. When the chen chi starts to develop, different people have different feelings. Most people feel warmth around the Dan Tian or vibrations in the Dan Tian area; some people can feel the chi circulating naturally around the small heavenly circle. But the most important point is that you don't try to push or force the chi before your chen chi is strong enough to circulate naturally around the small heavenly circuit. You must wait until it begins by itself. Trying to make the chi circulate around the small heavenly circuit before you are ready is like driving your car fast without gas or an oil change. It is bound to cause trouble.

- For new students, practice this set for three to five minutes. Once you have developed some skill, you can lengthen the duration of your practice bit by bit, up to a half hour or more.

- You should practice all of the exercises on both sides. This makes the Yin and Yang of the body well balanced and strengthens your physical body.

The standing exercises have three parts. The first part is the basic instructions you should follow throughout the entire set. The second part is how to move your arms and legs to get into the postures. The third part is how you should be moving internally in each posture, which you should work on after you can hold the posture. The internal instructions have been orally passed down from the Bagua masters in the form of poems, which we have included here. For each exercise, start with just the basic alignments in each posture; then, over time, add in the internal movements as described in the poems. Finally, work on the transitions, to make the practice smoother and more mindful.

The first set of exercises develops rooting with two legs, while the second set develops one-legged rooting skills. The two-legged standing set has eight movements, each with multiple techniques or uses. The one-legged standing set also has eight movements.

Two-Legged Chi Gong Exercises

Preparation Instructions and Poetry

Basic Instructions for All Standing Practices

The top of head goes up.

Take back your chin a little bit, to keep the neck straight.

Drop down your shoulders.

Relax your chest.

Breathe with your abdomen, feeling the movement in your belly, not your chest.

The toes grasp the ground, with natural relaxed strength.

Close your mouth, gently touch the roof of mouth with your tongue.

Concentrate your awareness on your Dan Tian.

Preparation Poem for All Standing Practices

This preparation poem tells you the principles of all the exercises to follow.

Standing, facing to the south,
Adjust your breathing, make it deep, slow, and even.
Focus your mind on your Dan Tian,
Feet shoulder width apart.
Toes gently grasp the ground.
Both arms and hands naturally hang down beside the thighs. The middle
*   finger is aligned with the "trouser crease."*
Whole body is naturally relaxed.
When you inhale and exhale, feel your Dan Tian.

Opening stance

Here are the eight postures.

Posture One: Dun, or Old Monk Holding the Bowl and Seven Stars Palm

- Bend both knees and drop your body weight.

- From this preparation, sink the body and legs and step forward with left foot into Ko Bu. Seventy percent of your weight is on the back leg.

- Lift both palms up and forward into Yang Zhang (lifting palms). The left palm is forward, the right palm is close to the left elbow. Pay attention to extending the fingers and palm strongly.

Poetry for Dun

Holding the seven stars, you extend your hands.
Your body stays back—don't lean forward to follow the palm and arm.
This is Cheng.
At the same time, both arms gently squeeze in together.
This is Guo.
Done together, they are called Cheng Guo.
When this is practiced, it develops a kind of strength or power called Li
  [in this case, Cheng Guo Li, which is the power of both expanding and
  contracting, or of extending and squeezing simultaneously].

The top of the head gently rises.

Draw back your chin a little, to help keep the neck straight.

Both shoulders relax.

This is called Ding.

The upper body is straight, with your chest slightly curved in and your back opening up, rounding, and expanding.

The hips are loose and relaxed.

The buttocks tuck under, and you gently close the anus and perineum.

With your lower body sitting down, bend both knees, with the thighs and knees slightly squeezing together.

This is Guo.

Between the upper and lower body the hip opens up and extends slightly, allowing the upper body to rise and the legs to sink.

This is Cheng Guo.

The function is to protect your groin and strengthen your root. Open Tiger Mouth.

Open up both palms strongly, with your eyes looking at your front palm.

At the same time, let your feet strongly sink into the ground.

Again, this is Cheng Guo.

Dun

These principle elements are a part of all eight postures, but are not mentioned each time. Be sure to put them in your practice.

Posture Two: Chi, or Horse Stance

- Draw back the right leg so you are standing in Bing Bu (one-footed stance). Then move your left foot out to the side in the Horse Stance.

- At the same time, bring both hands in toward your chest, your palms facing the body. Then extend your palms out in front of body, palms facing out.

Poetry for Chi

Bend the knees, until your hips are at knee height.
Turn both feet gently in, so they are parallel.
Turn both knees in slightly as well [gently!].
Open the Tiger Mouth Palms as large as you can,
Your fingers point to each other.
Your eyes look forward.
Both feet are pressed solidly into the ground.
Both arms are at shoulder height.
Focus your attention on your Dan Tian and empty your mind.

Chi

Posture Three: Gong, or Forward Stance

- Both hands raise up toward the sky in Gong Bu.

- From the Horse Stance, take back the right foot into Bing Bu. Then continue to move the right foot back into left Gong Bu.

- At the same time, both palms draw back until they are under your chin, facing up. Then, extend both palms out to the side, facing up as you step into Gong Bu. This is known as Tuo Tian Zhang.

Poetry for Gong

Bend the front knee, but don't bring it past the front toe.
The back foot is planted solidly on the ground.
Both arms extend out, at shoulder level.
Open the Tiger Mouth as widely as you can.
Extend your fingers strongly out to the side.
Relax your shoulders and let them sink down.
Your elbows should be relaxed.
The top of your head goes up, while your upper body is straight.

Gong

Posture Four: Pu, also called Pu Twei Yu Shen, or Scooping the Moon from the Ocean.

- Take the right foot and move it forward into Bing Bu.

- Move your weight to the right leg and sink down, bending the left knee very much, until you're really squatting down.

- Extend your left leg out to the left side, into Pu Bu.

- At the same time, both hands drop back in front of the ribs. Then extend your left palm toward the left foot, following the line of the body. Your palm is turned up, with the elbow facing up. The right palm moves back into Cheng Zhang, pushing back with the palm at shoulder height as you move in the other direction.

Poetry for Pu

Bend the right knee, extending the left leg.
Top of head goes up, body straight.
Left foot turns in a little bit, similar to Ko Bu.
Both arms extend strongly away from body.
Your eyes follow your right palm, then look to left palm at the end.
The whole movement is like "scooping the moon from the ocean."

Pu

Posture Five: Kou, or Lion Opens His Mouth

- Stand up into Bing Bu and take back the left foot next to the right. Both knees are naturally bent.

- Your left foot moves forward into Ko Bu from Bing Bu. This is called Chi Xing Bu or Seven Star Standing.

- At the same time, bring back your left palm to the chest, then extend it in front of your nose and straight up as far as you can. When you finish, your hand is straight up and your left shoulder is next to your ear. The arm is twisting strongly inward.

- As the left palm rises, the right palm drops down in front of the groin, then twists out and extends toward the right knee. The arm is twisting strongly outward.

Poetry for Kou

Bend both knees and squeeze in together.
The knees and the hips are at the same level, a very low stance. [Note: this is not supposed to hurt your legs, don't do more than you can safely do.]
Turn and twist both arms, elbows, and palms.
Extend both arms strongly, one up to sky, one down to earth.
Pay strong attention to your fingers.
Your body is straight, and your weight is on the back leg.
Your eyes look forward. Empty your mind.

Kou

Posture Six: Kou Bai, or Bai Bu Looking to the Side

- Your right leg stays in place.

- Your left leg moves to the left side in a big Bai Bu, until your left foot is on a sideways line with the right heel.

- At the same time, bend both knees down. Your body sinks down until the thighs are parallel to the ground (again, do not go lower than you can safely). Open up the hips.

- Your left palm pushes forward into Cheng Zhang with a gentle curve in the arm (it is not quite straight). The arms are also twisting. The fingers point sideways.

- Your right palm pushes down by the waist, with your fingers pointing to your side (Ta Zhang).

- Your eyes look over the left palm and beyond.

Poetry for Kou Bai

Left foot makes a big Bai Bu to the left side, heel to heel, sinking down, until the hip and knees are at the same level.
Both arms are a little bit bent and twisting.
Left palm pushes forward, right palm pushes back as hard as it can into Cheng Ta Zhang.
The top of the head goes up, the shoulder drops down, and the upper body is straight.
The weight is on both legs evenly.
Your toes grasp the ground strongly.
Your eyes move to left side,
*   following the left palm.*

Kou Bai

Posture Seven: Wo, or Body Sitting Down with Cross Step and Diagonal Flying Palm

- Your left foot moves back behind your right foot, crossing the legs, into the Wo stance.

- Your left palm turns up and pushes up into left Tuo Zhang.

- At the same time, your right hand pushes down.

- Both arms extend as much as they can. Your left arm goes higher than the top of the head. The right palm goes lower than your hip.

- Your head turns to the right, and your eyes look back and a bit down to the right side.

Poetry for Wo

Sit down on the back, or left leg, with left Wo Bu.
The left palm pushes up to the sky, like flying.
The right palm pushes down to earth.
Both arms are diagonal. Put equal strength in both arms.
Look back to your right palm, with your eyes strongly focused past the right
  arm, looking out to the horizon.

Wo

Posture Eight: Zuo, or Young Boy Prays to Buddha

- Sit down on the ground, with legs crossed Indian style.

- Both palms move in together in front of the chest, with your fingers up to sky, in He Bao Zhang or Holding Together Palms.

- Close your eyes.

Poetry for Zou

Sitting down with both legs crossed into Pan Xi.

The soles of the feet go to the sides and up [not too hard].

Both elbows are brought close together, along with the hands. Both arms squeeze together slightly.

The top of your fingers is at the height of your eyebrows.

Close your eyes slowly and gently, like the sun going down.

Your upper body is straight, the top your head is lifted.

Close your mouth, with your tongue gently touching the roof of mouth.

Your whole body is relaxed, with attention focused on the Dan Tian.

Zou

Closing Action

Stand up and uncross your legs into a regular standing posture, with your feet parallel and shoulder-width apart. As you begin to stand up, make a circle with both of your hands down, out, up, and in. As your palms move inward, they touch in front of your head and stay together until they reach in front of your chest, where they hold their position. Keep your attention on the Dan Tian and relax.

1

2

3

One-Legged Chi Gong Exercises

The preparation is the same as for the two-legged form.

Posture One: Chuo, or Pointing to Sky and Earth

- The left foot stays the same. Take the right foot and touch the toe close to the left foot, with the rest of the foot raised.

- At the same time, the left arm lifts straight up. Turn arm and palm outward, with fingers spearing toward the sky. The right palm turns outward, with fingers stretching down toward the earth. Eyes are looking forward.

Poetry for Chuo

Left leg is straight, the toes grasp the ground.
Right foot is straight, toes point straight down to earth.
Left arm close to left ear, right arm close to right hip. Both extend strongly.
Left palm up to sky, right palm down to earth, at the same time.
Body is kept straight, eyes looking straight forward.

Chuo

Posture Two: Li, or Keeping the Legs Straight (Dragon Diving into the Sea)

- Drop down your right foot, step forward with your left foot, and touch the ground with your left heel.

- Bend forward with the upper body, with both legs strying straight.

- Right palm presses down toward the inside of the left foot (alternately, you can grasp the sole of the left foot). Left palm stretches back with fingers pointing to the ground.

- Eyes keep looking forward (you will have to lift your head).

Poetry for Li

Both legs stay straight.
Right foot is planted, the left foot has the heel down and the toe up, seventy percent of the weight is on the right foot.
Both arms are extending, the right arm goes down to earth, the left one pushes up toward the sky.
Upper body leans forward, and your head lifts up to look forward.
Both palms push in balance with each other.

Li

Posture Three: Ti, or Single Leg Standing (Lifting Up Foot)

- Take back your left foot and lift up your right foot and leg, with your right toes pointed forward.

- Extend both arms to the side, palms pushing up to sky.

- Eyes look forward.

Poetry for Ti

Left leg is straight, grasping the ground with toes.
Lift up the right knee so it is parallel to your hip.
Toes of right foot point forward.
Body is straight.
Both palms push up to sky, fingers stretch outward.

Ti

Posture Four: Mian, or Turning In the Foot

- Left foot stays in place.

- Right foot turns in to protect groin. The sole of the foot is just off of the leg and knee.

- Left fingertips drop down to point toward the right foot. Right fingers stretch up to the sky and turn in, so your palm is facing backwards with your right elbow near your right ear.

- Eyes looking forward.

Poetry for Mian

Left leg standing straight and grasping ground with toes.
Keep right knee at hip level, right foot turns into Mian.
Body is straight.
Left fingers point down to earth through the right foot.
Right fingers point up to sky.

Mian

Posture Five: Pan, or Sitting Down on One Leg with Bent Knees

- Sink down on your left leg, with all your weight still on the left foot. Cross your right foot over your left knee.

- Both hands are positioned as if holding a ball in front of your chest. This is called Bao Zhang, or the tree hugger pose.

- Your eyes look forward.

Poetry for Pan

Bend the left knee and cross the right foot over the left knee.
Both hands move into Bao Zhang. Arms are held at shoulder height.
Chest is relaxed, back is rounded, spine is lifted up.
Eyes look forward, upper body is straight, top of head goes up.

Pan

Posture Six: Zhe, or Bending (Bending Knees with Palms Pushing Out)

- Maintain bend in left knee.

- Right foot moves behind your left knee, your body sitting down on your left leg.

- Both palms push out, with fingers facing each other.

- Your eyes look forward.

Poetry for Zhe

Bend the left knee and the right knee, right foot behind left knee.
The right foot and leg put pressure on the back of the left knee and leg.
Top of head goes up, neck and body are straight. Lower body sinks down.
Arms are held at shoulder height, with palms pointing out.

Zhe

Posture Seven: Deng, or Kicking to Front with Heel (Metal Body Bridge with Face Up)

- Left leg stays the same, bent with the weight of body on it.

- The upper body leans back with your face upward.

- Your right foot kicks forward with the heel, with both palms pushing back above your head.

Poetry for Deng

Arms raised like a big yawn.
Left leg is bent and grasping with toes.
Right leg is straight and extending out with the heel.
Your body leans back, looking up to the sky.
Hands and feet push in opposite directions, making it balanced.

Deng

Deng (side view)

Posture Eight: Chuai, or Stretching Back with Leg and Heel (Duck Swimming)

- Left leg stays in the same position.

- Right leg stretches backward with the heel.

- Both hands stretch forward, with eyes looking forward.

- Body leans forward.

Poetry for Chuai

Left leg is bent, and toes grasp the ground.
Right leg stretches back with the heel.
Body leans forward, like a swimming duck.
Both palms stretching forward,
Hands and feet push in opposite directions to make it balanced.

Chuai   Chuai (side view)

Closing Standing Movement

- Drop down your right foot to regular standing.

- As your feet come together and you stand up, bring your hands up and to the side, then overhead. Then bring them down in front of your body, ending with both palms in front of your Dan Tian, leading the chi there.

1

2

3

Chapter Five

Twenty-Four Movements of the Eight Animals

The traditional name for this form is "Twenty-Four Techniques of Small Movement of Eight Animals." This form is one of the treasured applications of South District Beijing Bagua Zhang, passed to the fifth generation from Master Wang Wen Kui. This form includes twenty-four movements of eight animals, starting on the Kun Gua (southwest corner) of the Bagua circle. The animal that is associated with the Kun Gua is the chilin (a mythical Chinese animal). The second one is the lion, on the Chian Gua (northwest corner). The third one is the bear, located on the Gen Gua (northeast corner). The fourth one is the phoenix, on the Xun Gua (southeast corner). The fifth one is the rooster, located on the Li Gua (south side). The sixth one is the monkey, located on the Dui Gua (west side). The seventh one is the snake, on the Kan Gua (north side). The eighth one is the dragon, located on the Zhen Gua (east side). The eight animals can be divided into two parts: the four animals located on the corners of the circle and the four animals located on the four directions. (See picture of the Bagua map and animals on page 32.)

Chi Xing Bu, or Seven Stars Stepping

The foundation stepping pattern for this form is called Seven Stars Stepping, or Chi Xing Bu. I'll explain how to practice it.

- You always start with the outside foot, Ko Bu. For example, when you first arrive at the Kun Gua, you are moving in the Yin direction, so your outside foot is your right foot. So you start with a right Ko Bu, and then a left Bai Bu, with your body sitting down on the back leg and opening the hips.

- The third step is an "over Ko Bu," a Ko Bu step in which the front foot finishes farther over the line made by the toes of the back foot. Here, the right foot finishes with its heel in line with the left toes. Your weight is on the left foot and you continue to look to the right side, over the right shoulder. The rest of your body is twisting to the left. Your hips and legs squeeze together tightly.

- In the fourth step, you bring your left leg around and behind your right foot, and step back into a cross stance, or Tsuo Bu. The weight is on the left leg, your right toe points out, and your hips are very open. Look back.

- In the fifth step, the right foot moves forward to the left foot and the right toe touches the middle of the inside of the left foot. Squeeze the thighs and knees tightly. Your weight is on the right leg.

- For the sixth step, the left foot steps forward into Shun Bu, and your body turns to the left and relaxes. Look forward.

- For the seventh step, step forward with the right leg into a small Ko Bu. Your weight is on the left foot. Then, the body twists to the center of the circle, while sinking down with bent knees. But the top of your head stays lifted up. Keeping your head lifted the whole time is very important for strengthening the body, especially the spine.

Walk

1

2

3

4

5

6   7

This is the Seven Stars Stepping pattern, the foundation stepping pattern of the Twenty-Four Movements of Eight Animals form. Of course, some of the individual movements vary from this pattern, but they are all based on the Seven Star Stepping. The function of this pattern is to coil and uncoil the body with each step. This strengthens your muscles and tendons, creates a large range of motion, and increases the circulation of chi and blood. This in turn supports your health and develops the coiling power of the body. The second function of this stepping pattern is to develop good balance while your body is moving and turning. The third function is to strengthen and improve the function of your peripheral and central nervous system. This improves your coordination and timing and creates good body awareness. The fourth function is to strengthen and massage the internal organs, as the twisting and untwisting massages and energizes the internal organs.

The Seven Star Stepping pattern is based on the Shuang Bai Shuang Ko stepping pattern, and is something that I have developed. When Master Wang Wen Kui taught this form to the students, he used the three-step style. The three-step style starts with a Ko Bu with the outside foot (the right), then Bai Bu with the inside foot (the left), and finishes with the right foot stepping forward into Shun Bu. The three-step style is easier to learn and to practice than the Seven Star Stepping pattern, and it gives students a good foundation. The Seven Star Stepping pattern is more difficult but has more health benefits and applications.

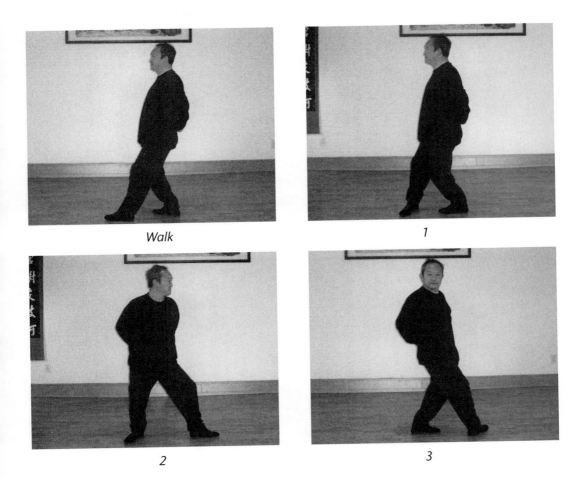

Walk

1

2

3

There is also a five-step style. It starts with right foot Ko Bu, then left foot Bai Bu, right foot over Ko Bu, left foot Tsuo Bu, and ends with right foot Shun Bu. That finishes the circle with five steps instead of seven, but the body movement is the same. The body and palm movements for the three-step style are a bit simpler than the five- or seven-step methods, but they are the same in essence. When you practice this form, you should first learn the three-step style, and then you can learn the seven-step style. The five-step method is the most difficult and should be practiced only after the other two methods have been learned well.

Walk

1

2

3

4

5

Standing Chi Gong Preparation for the Circle Walk

- You start from the Chian Gua of the Bagua circle. Stand relaxed, facing south.

- Lift up both arms with palms down and inhale, until both arms are at the level of the shoulders.

- Relax the left shoulder and extend the left arm, until the chi and blood extend out to the fingertips. Your eyes are looking toward the left hand. Repeat the same movement with the right arm.

- Then look forward with both arms extending and raising up until they are completely above your head, palms up. Your palms push up and stretch out your whole body.

- Relax your shoulders as you exhale, turn left as you inhale, and grasp the ground harder with your toes as your whole body twists and stretches. Your body then turns back to the front as you exhale. Repeat the same movement on the right side.

- Then drop down both arms to your Dan Tian in an S pattern, moving first to the left and then to the right as they drop down.

- You finish with both hands pressing down in front of your Dan Tian, with your fingers facing each other in a Tiger Mouth position. The top of your head goes up, but the rest of your body is sinking down. Take back your chin a bit and straighten your neck. Your eyes keep looking forward. Your shoulders are slightly curved, your chest sinks, and your back rounds. Close your mouth and place the tip of your tongue on your palate. This is the same as the opening chi gong for the circle walk. (See page 66 for photos.)

Start walking on the circle counterclockwise, starting with the inside foot. This is the Yin direction of the Bagua circle. Do a complete circle, and then continue on until you get to the Kun Gua.

At that point, you start to practice the three movements of the chilin.

Chilin

First Form: Chilin Pushes Down to the Earth

Walking: Press palms down in front of the body, your palms facing the floor, your fingers facing each other. Elbows are out and shoulders are rounded. Look forward (1).

- Start with your left foot inside, walking (Yin direction) with your eyes looking forward.

- Right Ko Bu. Keeping your palms down, twist your hands out until your fingers point outward, sixty to ninety degrees. Elbows twist inward. Torso and head remain looking forward (2).

- Left Bai Bu. Turn palms back, then inward as you continue to twist your arms. Elbows stay down, torso and head face backward. Hands end with fingers facing both sides of the waist, on the belt channel, called the Dai Mai points (3).

- Right Guo Ko Bu. Palms lift up to underneath chin. Then, continue to push up with your palms as high as you can, fingers pointing at each other, palms up. Body twists to the left. At this point, the whole body is twisting, extending, and strongly sinking down with the legs and body. Eyes keep looking in the Yang direction (4).

- Left Tsuo Bu. Palms keep lifting up as high as they will go, with elbows in, arms twisting, and fingers pointing forward and out. Your body twists to the left, your eyes look in the Yin direction (5).

- Right withdrawing step. Palms stay up and twist inward, until the fingers are facing each other again. Elbows out. Your body twists to the left, eyes looking in the Yang direction (6).

- Left Shun Bu. Turn your body and arms together with the step. Head and eyes look in the Yang direction (7).

- Right Shang Bu (8).

- Palms drop down to the walking position (9).

- Shuang Ta Zhang. From the walking position, the whole body presses down through the hands, in a quick and strong movement. This is internal strength, using the whole body to create power without any large motions of the joints or body.

1

2

3

4

5

6

7

8

9

Second Form: Chilin Shoulders Mountain

Walking: Fingers point backwards toward the shoulders, palms facing up. For beginners, you can point the fingers out a bit, but keep the palms in front of the shoulders. The elbows are down and in front of the body. The forearms are kept parallel and close together (1).

- Right Ko Bu. Keeping your hands at the same height, twist your forearms outward and around, until you have crossed your right forearm over your left. Palms end facing inward toward your shoulders, while the arms are twisting and pressing outward. The elbows are pointing down and a bit out. Torso, head, and eyes face in the Yin direction (2).

- Left Bai Bu. Keep twisting your forearms and turn your hands over, so the forearms scissor and the palms are facing outward. The palms and forearms push out and your chest is in, so the arms and the torso are moving away from each other with a feeling of expanding. The elbows are pointed out. Head and eyes face in the Yang direction (3).

- Right Guo Ko Bu. Raise your palms up above your head and push up with elbows out. Your torso turns to the left, while your head and eyes look back past the outside of your arm in the Yin direction (4).

- Left Tsuo Bu. Hold arm posture. Body is twisting, extending, and the legs and torso are strongly sinking and closing. Eyes look in the Yin direction (5).

- Right withdrawing step. Hold arm posture. Eyes looking in Yang direction (6).

- Left Shun Bu. Hold arm posture. Eyes looking in Yang direction (7).

- Right Shuang Bu. Bring elbows around to front of the body, and then drop elbows and palms back into walking form (8).

- Shuang He Zhang. From the walking position, sink down with your body and press your forearms together, while keeping your hands in the same posture. Do this quickly and while exhaling.

1

2

3

4

5

6

7   8

Third Form: Chilin Pushes Up to the Sky

Walking form: Raise palms high up overhead, facing up with fingers facing each other. Elbows are out and up, shoulders are down (1).

- Right Ko Bu. Move your elbows around and in front of you, so your forearms touch each other in front of your chest. Palms face back. Body and eyes face the Yin direction (2).

- Left Bai Bu. Move your elbows out and rotate the forearms so the palms face out in front of you at shoulder height, fingertips just touching. Palms push forward strongly, with the body keeping back. Look in the Yang direction with head and eyes (3).

- Right Guo Ko Bu. Raise your palms up into the walking form. Eyes look back past the outside of your arms in the Yang direction. Arms and body are twisting and extending, and the legs are closing and sinking (4).

- Left Tsuo Bu. Hold arm posture. Eyes look in the Yin direction (5).

- Right withdrawing step. Hold arm posture. Eyes look in the Yang direction (6).

- Left Shun Bu. Hold arm posture. Eyes and head look in the Yang direction (7).

- Right Xu Bu. Bring your right foot next to your left foot, with the ball of the right foot just touching the ground. Hold arm posture.

- Right Gen Bu. Take a small step forward with your right foot, then "follow step" with your left foot, bringing it closer behind the right foot. Hold arm posture and press palms up strongly just as you finish the Gen Bu. The feeling is of transferring your forward momentum to upward pushing. Extend the arms upward as you sink down with your legs (8).

1

2

3

4

5

6

7

8

Foundation Practice and Advanced Practice

When you are first practicing the chilin, you look in the direction you are walking and your arms are in front of you. This helps to develop good body alignment and extension. After you have practiced the chilin for six months or so, you can switch to the more advanced version, in which you look to the center of the circle and both of your arms face in instead of forward, as you do in the finishing movement of the chilin. This creates more twisting strength. When your body turns in to the center, it is important that your steps stay in the same position—you need to create the twisting in your waist and body, not your legs. You do this for all three of the chilin forms, at the finish of the change.

Basic walk

Advanced walk

Lion

First Form: Lion Holds the Ball

Walking: Walk in the Yin direction, with your left foot inside. Eyes and head look to the center of the circle. Left palm is in front of hip with palm up, elbow back. Right palm is in front of the left shoulder with palm facing down, elbow out in front of body. You can imagine that you are holding a ball in your two hands as you walk (1).

- Right Ko Bu. Imagine that you are holding a ball. Rotate the ball one-eighth of a turn, while you keep facing the center of the circle (2).

- Left Bai Bu. While still holding the ball, rotate it another one eighth of a turn. Keep looking to the center (3).

- Right Gou Ko Bu. Turn the ball another one quarter of a turn; your hands are now in the opposite position from when you started the change. Look in the Yang direction over your right shoulder. Your body and arms are extending and twisting, while the legs are sinking and closing (4).

- Left Tsuo Bu. Hold your arm position and look in the Yin direction (5).

- Right withdrawing step. Hold your arm position and look in the Yang direction with eyes and head (6).

- Left Shun Bu. Hold your arm position and keep looking in the Yang direction (7).

- Right Ko Bu. Hold your arm position and look to the outside of the circle with head and eyes. Again, your body is strongly twisting and sinking. The top of the head goes up (8).

- Hooking kick step. Quickly twist your head, shoulders, and waist to the inside, while raising your right leg up and forty-five degrees outside the circle (9).

- Kick forty-five degrees out of the circle with your right foot, using the outside of the foot to kick. Then step down and walk in the Yang direction (10).

1

2

3

4

5

6

7

8

9

10

Second Form: Lion Grasps the Ball

Walking: Walk in the Yin direction, eyes forward. Hands are out in front of your body, facing down, with elbows facing down. Imagine that you're holding a big ball underwater or that you're pressing down with both palms (1).

- Right Ko Bu. As you step, both palms make a circle in front of your body, so that your hands end up fingers out and palms up at waist height, in front of your body. Keep looking forward (2).

- Left Bai Bu. Pull your hands toward your Dai Mai (the belt meridian), then slide them palm up around the Dai Mai until the sides of the palms touch the sides of your body. Palms are still up. Look in the Yang direction (3).

- Right Guo Ko Bu. Keep pulling your hands back until they're behind you at the Ming Men point (back near the kidneys), then point the fingers to each other, palms still facing up at waist height. Keep looking in the Yang direction over the right shoulder (4).

- Left Tsuo Bu. Draw the palms as far back as you can, then draw them out to the side and swing them around in front of you, finishing in the walking posture. The palms stay facing up until the end, when the shoulders and arms twist so the elbows and palms are facing down. Head and eyes look in the Yin direction (5).

- Right withdrawing step. Hold arm position. Head and eyes look in the Yang direction (6).

- Left Shun Bu. Hold arm position, keep looking in the Yang direction (7).

- Right Xu Bu. Hold arm position.

- Right Gen Bu. As you do the follow step, press down with the palms, withdraw them toward your belly, then curl them up near your chest. Quickly finish the follow step so you land and sink down just as your hands return to the walking position (8, 9).

1

2

3

4

5

6

7

8

9

Third Form: Rolling Lion

Walking form: Walk in the Yin direction, palms facing forward, fingers pointed toward each other in front of chest. Elbows face out, looking in the Yin direction (1).

- Right Ko Bu. Turn palms and arms so that your right elbow is facing up, with your right fingers facing down and pointing at the left fingers, which point up. The left elbow is down. Look in the Yang direction. Palms are still in front of your body (2).

- Left Bai Bu. Both palms move to face downward in front of the hips, and you are strongly pushing down. Head and eyes look in the Yang direction (3).

- Right Guo Ko Bu. Bring both palms in front of the body and then above your head. The arms are moving in a vertical circle. Fingers keep facing each other. Head and eyes keep looking in the Yang direction, past the right shoulder and arm (4).

- Start by lifting the left knee up high and tight, and then step into left Pu Bu. Your palms move in front of your body, fingers pointing at each other. Right elbow up, left elbow down. Head and eyes look in the Yin direction (5).

- Right withdrawing step. Palms move to face downward. Head and eyes look in the Yang direction (6).

- Left Shun Bu. Both palms move in front of the body, facing down. Look in the Yang direction (7).

- Right Shang Bu. Palms and body twist so they are facing outside the circle with the palms at chest height. Then, twist your body to face the center, while the palms press up overhead and then press toward the center. Eyes and head follow the hands. Then bring your palms in front of your body, facing in the Yang direction (8).

- Shuang Tui Zhang. Explosively press forward with both hands, while your body stays back. Then begin to walk the other way (9).

1   2

3

4

5

6

7

8

9

10

Foundation and Advanced Practice

When you first start learning the lion, you face the direction you are walking, and at the end you press forward. After about six months of practicing the lion, you should be ready to twist your body so that your palms can face the center of the circle, and you press into the circle. Again, this foundation practice emphasizes body alignment and extension, and the advanced method has more twisting in it.

Bear

First Form: Bear Looking Back

Walking form: Walk in the Yin direction and look to the center of the circle. Your left palm is behind your kidneys, facing backward, with fingers horizontal. Your right palm is in front of your forehead, facing forward, with the fingers horizontal. Both arms are twisting and extending about seventy percent (1).

- Right Ko Bu. Strongly extend both hands and look backward in the Yang direction. The palms move with the body (2).

- Left Bai Bu. Keep extending your arms and keep turning. Keep your arms moving with your body. Keep looking in the Yang direction (3).

- Right Guo Ko Bu. Keep extending, keep turning. Keep looking in the Yang direction over your right shoulder and arm. Arms and body are extending and twisting, legs are sinking and closing (4).

- Left Tsuo Bu. Keep extending, keep turning. Look in the Yin direction (5).

- Right withdrawing step. Keep extending, keep twisting. Look in the Yang direction (6).

- Left Shun Bu. Keep extending, keep looking in the Yang direction (7).

- Right Shang Bu. Turn palms to face in and bring them together, with the right palm passing just over the left palm in front of your chest, with the fingers parallel to each other. From there, extend your arms out into the walking position, with your left arm in front and your right arm behind. Look back to the Yin direction (8).

- Tui/Ta Zhang. Extend your palms away from body (101%!) as you sink your weight into your legs. Look back in the Yin direction as you extend, then look to the center and bring your arms back to seventy percent extended as you start walking in the Yang direction.

1

2

3

4

5

6

7

8

Second Form: Bear Holds Up Sun and Moon

Walking form: Walk in the Yin direction, looking forward. Your left palm is facing down with fingers pointing at the waist. Your right palm is facing up, with fingers pointing to the right temple. Both elbows are facing to the side, and both shoulders are dropped (1).

- Right Ko Bu. Strongly extend palms up and down (101%), looking to the center of the circle. Your body is sinking down a little bit (2).

- Left Bai Bu. Keep extending your arms up and down. Look in the Yang direction (3).

- Right Guo Ko Bu. Same as step number two (4).

- Left Tsuo Bu. The same, but look in the Yin direction (5).

- Right withdrawing step. The same, but look in the Yang direction (6).

- Left Shun Bu. Keep looking in the Yang direction (7).

- Right Shang Bu. Turn palms over and bring them in front of your chest, with the right palm inside the left palm, both palms facing in. Then turn your palms up and down, this time with the right palm down and the left palm up. Look to the center of the circle (8).

- To/An Zhang. Extend palms up and down strongly, while sinking the weight into the legs. Then begin walking in the Yang direction. Keep looking to the center of the circle (9).

1

2

3

4

5

6

7

8

9

Third Form: Bear Pierces Earth and Sky

Walking form: Walk in the Yin direction, looking forward. Your right fingers are pointing up above your shoulder, your palm facing out. Your left fingers are pointing down, your palm facing in. Both arms completely extend vertically, shoulders down (1).

- Right Ko Bu. Strongly extend fingers up and down. Look to the center of the circle (2).

- Left Bai Bu. Keep extending. Look back (3).

- Right over Ko Bu. Keep extending. Keep looking back (4).

- Left Tsuo Bu. Keep extending. Look forward (5).

- Right withdrawing step. Keep extending. Look backward (6).

- Left Shun Bu. Keep looking back (7).

- Right Shang Bu. Turn your fingers to point toward each other, then bring them together in front of your chest, passing the backs of the palms as they move to reverse positions. Finish with your right fingers pointing down, your palm facing the center of the circle. Your left fingers are pointing up, your palm facing out (8).

- Fa Jin. Extend your fingers up and down strongly, and twist your left hand so the palm faces outside the circle. Sink your weight into your legs, then begin walking in the Yang direction.

1

2

3

4

5

6

7

8

Phoenix

First Form: Phoenix Folds Wings Back

Walking form: Walk in the Yin direction of the circle, eyes facing forward, with both arms down at your sides and your fingers swept down and backwards (1).

- Right Ko Bu. Look outside the circle. Extend your hands out to your sides, with your left hand back and your front hand forward, then swing them both toward the outside of the circle. Then the right arm twists and goes forward to protect your forehead. Your inside or left palm twists and goes back to protect your back, by the Ming Men point. Your eyes follow the right palm going out and forward, then look back (2).

- Left Bai Bu. Keep looking back as your arms move with your body. Keep your hands close to your head and body, partially coiled (3).

- Right over Ko Bu. Keep looking back in the Yang direction, over your right shoulder. Maintain arms. The top of your head is rising up while your legs are sinking down (4).

- Left Tsuo Bu. Open hips as both feet turn out and you sit down on the left leg. Look in the Yin direction and maintain your arms (5).

- Right withdrawing step. Look in the Yang direction and continue to coil the arms (6).

- Left Shun Bu. Keep looking in the Yang direction, arms coiling around with body.

- Right Shang Bu to little Ko Bu. Ma Mien Zhang, or "wash the face side to side." This means that you use your hand to "wash" the other person's face. You should be very close to them when you do this, and you use your legs and waist to create "washing power." Your body twists toward the outside of the circle, looking to the outside of the circle. At this time, your hands should be very close to your forehead and Ming Men point. They should have been moving gradually closer and coiling more and more. At the end, quickly extend both palms in the direction of their movement (7).

- Then, look to the inside of the circle and bring both hands in front of your body, palms facing down. Then bring your fingers in toward the Dai Mai as you face in the Yang direction. Then point your fingers out in front of you at shoulder height as your raise your right knee.

- Transition kick straight out with your toe as you slice down and back, with both hands returning to the walking form. Then take back your foot and start walking in the Yang direction (8,9).

1

2

3

4

5

6

7

7 (outside view)

8

9

Second Form: Phoenix Starts to Open Wings

Walking form: Walk in the Yin direction of the circle, eyes facing forward, with both arms at your side and extending out at forty-five degrees. Fingers point out to the side and down, with palms down (1).

- Right Ko Bu. Look to the center of the circle. Bring your right hand down and in front of your groin, with fingers facing down. This protects your groin. Bring your left hand up above and in front of your head, with your palm facing out and fingers pointing sideways (2).

- Left Bai Bu. Keep looking to the center of the circle. Extend your right hand, palm out, toward the center of the circle, with the palm facing the center, fingers sideways to left side of body. This is Heng Tui Zhang. Your left palm pushes up above your head, with your fingers pointing to the right side of your body (3).

- Right over Ko Bu. Look backward over your right shoulder. This is the same posture as the third step of the second and third chilin form. Palms face the sky, with fingers pointing toward each other (4).

- Left Tsuo Bu. Look forward. Maintain arms (5).

- Right withdrawing step. Look backward. Maintain arms (6).

- Left Shun Bu. Keep looking backward. Arms rotate with the body.

- Right Shang Bu. Look outside the circle and behind you. Both hands chop vertically down behind you to waist height, using the edge of the palm. Your body sinks down as you chop (7).

- Then look to the middle of the circle and extend your arms toward the middle of the circle, with your palms facing outward (8).

- Then do "Flower under Leaves" as you look behind you (9).

- Transition. Lift your right knee up and twist your leg toward the outside of the circle, preparing for a hooking foot kick (10).

- At the same time, look to the inside of the circle, and sweep your hands down and out, into the walking form posture. As you do this, your body turns toward the center of the circle. Then, your right foot kicks forward and out of the circle with your toe in a hooking motion (11).

1

2

3

4

5

6

- Draw back your foot (12).

- And then step with your right foot to begin walking.

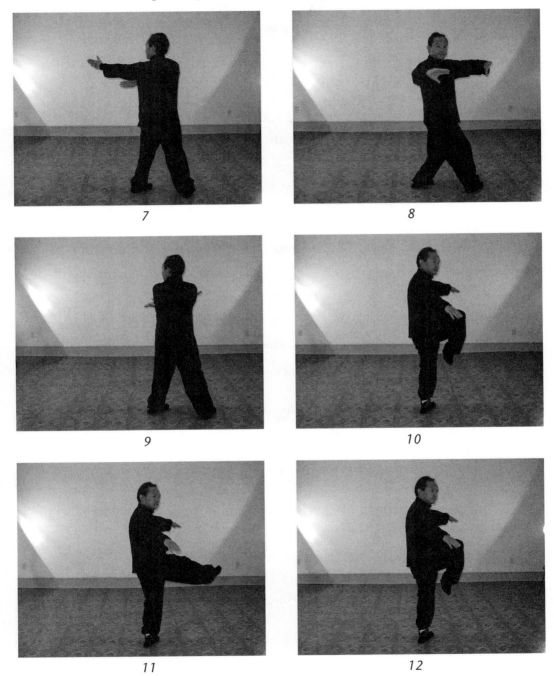

7

8

9

10

11

12

Third Form: Phoenix Flying

Walking form: Walk in the Yin direction, head and eyes looking to the center of the circle. Fingers are extended out to either side of your body at shoulder height, with palms down (1).

- Right Ko Bu. Keep looking to the center of the circle. Extend right fingers straight down toward the toes. This protects the groin. Extend left fingers straight up. Both palms face the middle of the circle. The upper palm is directly above the lower palm, and both are fully extended (2).

- Left Gung Bu. Extend your right palm out in front of the face, fingers pointed to the middle of the circle. This is Chuan Zhang, or striking with the fingers. Your right palm extends up above your head, the same as with the second form. Keep looking to the center of the circle (3).

- Right over Ko Bu. Look back over your right shoulder. Bring your hands above your head, with the backs of your palms touching. The arms are extending and the fingers are pointing straight up (4).

- Left Tsuo Bu. Look forward. Maintain arms (5).

- Right withdrawing step. Look backward over the left shoulder. Maintain arms (6).

- Left Shun Bu. Keep looking backward. Arms move with the body (7).

- Right Shang Bu. Look to the center of the circle. Extend your arms out to the sides with the palms up, then down with the palms inward, then crossing the arms with the palms down, then raising the arms above your head with palms facing inward. Then drop your arms to shoulder height, with the palms facing up (8).

- Both of your arms are making a large circle in front of your body. At the finish of the movement, quickly extend out with both arms and turn the palms over, so they are facing down. This is called Tan Zhang (9).

- Inside circle step. Make a little Bai Bu with your right foot, then make four small steps to make a small inside circle. Palms are down and extended out to the sides. In total, you make five steps. Finish with another right Ko Bu, your head facing the center of the circle. Your upper body and face are turned into the center of the circle. Both of your arms are strongly extending to each side. Then, make a Tan Zhang with both hands as you sink down strongly. This is a strong, short, and quick movement. Even though you are sinking down strongly, the top of your head lifts up (10).

- Then continue walking in the Yang direction on the circle.

1

2

3

4

5

6

7

8

9

10

Rooster

First Form: Rooster Bends Wings

Walking form: Walk in the Yin direction on the circle. Your right palm is in front of your left hip, with fingers extended down and the palm facing to the center of the circle. The left palm is in front of your right shoulder, with fingers pointed up and the palm facing outside the circle. Both palms squeeze and push away from each other, opening up the shoulders. Your eyes look at a 45-degree angle off of your line of sight to the center of the circle (1).

- Right standing posture. Look forward. Stand up tall on your right leg, with your left knee raised high in front of your body, toes pointed down. The left palm turns over to face you, fingers pointed up, with the elbow right in front of your solar plexus and your arms are twisting. This is called Yan Zhang. (Yan means "protect.") Your right palm lifts up so it is beneath the left elbow, fingers facing the middle of the circle. This is called Tuo Zhang, which means to push up (2).

- Left Bai Bu. Look back. As you step down into Bai Bu, you pivot slightly on the right heel to get into the posture. Sweep your left hand down in front of your left leg, with the palm facing out and the fingers down. When you finish, your left hand should be just outside of your left knee, with the left arm straight. Raise your right arm back and up, so your upper arm is near your ear, and your right palm faces backwards with a twisting motion. The right fingers point straight up. The hands should have a strong feeling of extending and twisting, up and down. Your weight is sinking down into your right leg. This movement is called Sa Zhang. Sa means opening the net (like a fishing net) (3).

- Right over Ko Bu. Look to the outside of the circle. Your right arm stays straight, and you bring your palm down in front of your head but away from it. This is called Ma Mian Zhang, or up down palm. At the same time, your left palm protects your ribs, with the fingers sideways and the palm facing out (4).

- Left Tsuo Bu. Look back in the Yin direction. Extend both of your palms outward in front of your chest, fingers pointed toward each other. This is double punch palm or Shuang Tui Zhang (5).

- Right withdrawing step. Look in the Yang direction. Keep your body and arm position (6).

- Left Shun Bu. While looking in the Yang direction, keep your body and arm position (7).

- Right Ko Bu. Look to the outside of the circle. Step with your right foot into a small Ko Bu. Body and arms keep their basic position, with palms facing outside the circle (8).

- Then lift your hands over your head and bring them down to the other side, with palms facing up and fingers pointing out. This is called Shuai Zhang or back of palm strike (9).

- As you strike, sink down with your legs to create power. Then return to the posture of move one, on the opposite side (10).

- Transition. Toe kick forward, draw your foot back, and then begin to walk in the Yang direction while keeping your hand position (11).

1   2

3

4

5

6

7

8

9

10

11

Second Form: Golden Rooster Crows in the Morning

Walking form: Walk in the Yin direction, looking to the center of the circle through the space between your thumb and index finger. Your left hand is facing the center of the circle, similar to the single palm change posture, except that the palm is more extended out, with the palm facing right to the center of the circle. This is called cow's tongue or Niu She Zhang. Your right palm is pressing down, just outside of your right hip. The right fingers are pointed to the hip (1).

• Right Ko Bu. Eyes look in the Yin direction. Bring your left palm in front of your face to above your right shoulder, with the palm facing out, fingers sideways. The right palm folds under the left elbow, also with the palm out, fingers sideways. This is the same as the single palm change (2).

- Left Bai Bu. Eyes look in the Yang direction. Keep your body and arm position. This is also like the single palm (3).

- Right over Ko Bu. Keep looking in the Yang direction. Keep your body and arm position (4).

- Left Tsuo Bu. Look in the Yin direction. Keep your body and arm position (5).

- Right withdrawing step. Look in the Yang direction. Keep your body and arm position (6).

- Left Shun Bu. Keep looking in the Yang direction (7).

- Right follow step. Take a small step forward with your left foot (8).

- Then take a full step with your right foot. As you bring your left foot up behind you (follow step), push out with the right palm (9).

- At the same time, your left palm withdraws a little to protect your chest and ribs. Look in the Yang direction, the same direction you are moving.

- Left follow step. Repeat follow step on other side. Push out with your left palm as you finish the step, the same as before (10).

- Right follow step. Repeat follow step again. Push out with your right palm as you finish the step (11).

- Right half follow step. Lunge forward with your right foot, then bring your left foot up behind. This is the half follow step. At the same time, quickly extend your arms into the walking form, looking to the center of the circle. This is called Heng Kai Zhang, and needs to be very fast (12).

- Then begin walking in the Yang direction.

1

2

3

4

5

6

7

8

9

10

11

12

Third Form: Rooster Eating Rice

Walking form: Walk in the Yin direction of the circle, looking to the center of the circle over your left shoulder. Your left elbow is pointed forward at shoulder height, with your upper arm and palm facing the left shoulder. The fingers and thumb touch together at a point about three inches in front of the center of the palm. This is called Guo Shou, or bringing the fingers of the hand together. This resembles the "beak" of the rooster. The left hand is twisting in, so it points to the center of the circle. The right arm is down by your right side, behind the right hip, in the same "beak" position, but the hand and fingers are twisting so the fingers point to the outside of the circle (1).

- Right Ko Bu. Drop down your left Guo Shou and bend the elbow, so it points to your left collarbone and your Chue Pen point. At the same time, lift your right wrist straight upward while keeping your fingers down. This is a strike with the back of the wrist. At the same time, sink down strongly onto your left leg while looking in the Yin direction (2).

- Left Bai Bu. Drop both Guo Shou to just underneath your armpit, with fingers facing straight back. Then extend both arms backwards, as you sink down onto the right leg. Look in the Yang direction (3).

- Right over Ko Bu. Your body leans far to the left side, optimally at a 90-degree angle with the ground. (This is a difficult maneuver.) Your right arm goes over your head and extends, fingers pointing outside the circle. The left Guo Shou is under your right armpit, protecting your ribs. Your eyes look outside the circle (4).

- Left Tsuo Bu. Both arms extend out to the sides with the fingers twisting back, so the fingers are facing in the Yang direction. Your eyes look in the Yin direction (5).

- Right withdrawing step. Look in the Yang direction and keep your arms in position with your body (6).

- Left Shun Bu. At the same time, the left arm circles over your head and goes forward, your fingers pointing outside the circle at shoulder height. The right hand stays behind the body, with the fingers pointing up (7).

- Continue looking in the Yang direction. Left Ko Bu. Your left foot steps forward into Ko Bu. At the same time, the right arm circles overhead and extends forward, with the fingers pointing to the center of the circle. The left hand goes behind the body, with the fingers pointing upward (8).

- Then the whole body twists, your hands return to the walking posture, and you look to the center of the circle through your right shoulder (9).

- Then continue to walk in the Yang direction.

1

2

3

4

5

6

7

8

9

Monkey

First Form: Monkey Holds Cauldron

Walking form: Walk in the Yin direction of the circle. Hold both hands out in front of your Dan Tian, palms facing in, fingers pointing toward each other, with the elbows pointing down and a little out. The feeling is of having your arms stretched out and a little down, as if you were holding a heavy cauldron (1).

- Ko Bu. Body, head, and eyes continue to face in the Yin direction. Draw your palms in toward your Dan Tian, until they just touch the body. The feeling is like you are pushing your chi into the Dan Tian (2).

- Bai Bu. Turn your body, head, and eyes to the Yang direction. While keeping your hands in the same basic position, move your fingers around the Dai Mai until they point to the side of your body (3).

- Right over Ko Bu. Your body turns toward the Yin direction, but the head and eyes keep looking in the Yang direction. Keep the same basic hand position, then bring your hands around the Dai Mai until they are behind your back, with the backs of the palms just touching the Ming Men points on the back. This movement moves the chi from the Dan Tian to the Ming Men points along the Dai Mai (4).

- Left Tsuo Bu. Your body, head, and eyes face in the Yin direction. Keep the same basic hand position, then pull the hands apart and bring them around so they are in the walking position again. Relax your shoulders and extend both arms as much as you can. When you finish, both hands should be in the walking posture. This movement gathers in the chi from nature and the environment (5).

- Right withdrawing step. Your body, head, and eyes turn in the Yang direction. Keep the same body and arm posture (6).

- Left Shun Bu. Your body, head, and eyes stay facing in the Yang direction. Keep the same body and arm posture (7).

- Right Shang Bu. Your body, head, and eyes stay facing in the Yang direction. Keep the same body and arm posture.

- Slowly bring your hands in toward your Dan Tian, as if you were squeezing the cauldron (8).

- When your hands just touch your body, slowly release your arms and return to the walking position (9).

1

2

3

4

5

6

7

8

9

Second Form: Five Flower Hand

Walking form: Walk in the Yin direction on the circle, holding both palms facing out in front of your Dan Tian. Your fingers are pointed outward, with a slight curve in the palms, and the wrists are just touching. Your eyes are looking in the Yin direction. Your arms squeeze together and your elbows are in close to your body (1).

- Right Ko Bu. Your body, head, and eyes continue to face in the Yin direction. Twist your hands around your wrists counterclockwise 180 degrees. The fingers keep extending as you twist. The axis of the rotation, or the root of the motion, is at the wrists (2).

- Left Bai Bu. Your body, head, and eyes turn to face in the Yang direction. Twist your hands around your wrists clockwise 360 degrees, again keeping the fingers extended and separated and the wrists touching, to form the axis of the rotation (3).

- Right over Ko Bu. Your head and eyes face in the Yang direction, but your body and waist turn in the Yin direction. Both hands start to turn down, with the back of the wrists touching and the palms facing outward. The elbows are down and a little out, and the hands are still in front of the Dan Tian (4).

- Left Tsuo Bu. Your body, head, and eyes are facing in the Yin direction. Both hands continue to twist around the wrists so the fingers point toward your Dan Tian. Your hands continue to touch at the back of the wrists (5).

- Right withdrawing step. Turn your body, head, and eyes to face in the Yang direction. Your fingers continue to rotate until they are pointing upward, still rotating around the wrists in front of your Dan Tian (6).

- Left Shun Bu. Keep your body, head, and eyes facing in the Yang direction. Continue to rotate your palms around your wrists until you return to the walking arm posture. Your elbows and upper arms are close in to your body, and the fingers are strongly extended and separated (7).

- Right Shang Bu. Keep your body, head, and eyes facing in the Yang direction (8).

- As you finish the step, sink down with your body as you extend your arms out in front of you quickly and strongly. Keep your elbows and wrists together as you extend your arms (9).

- Then begin walking in the Yang direction.

1

2

3

4

5

6

7

8

9

Third Form: Monkey Offers Fruit

Walking form: Walk in the Yin direction on the circle, your head and eyes facing in the Yin direction. Drop your shoulders and bring your elbows together in front of your Dan Tian. Touch the insides of your wrists together, close to your chin, with your fingers extending out in a "v" shape, a twenty-degree angle between them (1).

- Right Ko Bu. Your body, head, and eyes continue to face in the Yin direction. Extend your fingers and arms strongly out in the Yin direction. Keep your wrists touching and your elbows squeezed in as close as you can. Be sure to keep your weight on the left foot (the back leg) (2).

- Left Bai Bu. Your body, head, and eyes turn to face in the Yang direction. Bring your hands to your sides at waist level, and point your fingers at your Dai Mai with your palms up (3).

- Right over Ko Bu. Your body turns in the Yin direction, with your head and eyes facing in the Yang direction. Continue to move your hands around the Dai Mai until the back of the palms touch each other in back of the Ming Men points. The fingers point backwards and a little down (4).

- Left Tsuo Bu. Your body, head, and eyes face in the Yin direction. At the same time, both arms make a big circle in front of the body. Extend your arms and fingers as much as you can, and squeeze the forearms and wrists together. Your fingers face out at chin height with the palms up (5).

- Right withdrawing step. Your body, head, and eyes turn to face in the Yang direction. Bring your arms in toward your body, similar to the walking form (6).

- Left Shun Bu. Your body, head, and eyes keep facing in the Yang direction. Your arms keep their position (7).

- Right Shang Bu. Your body, head, and eyes keep facing in the Yang direction (8).

- As you finish your step, extend your arms strongly and quickly out in front of you, again at chin height (9).

- Then take back your arms into the walking position and begin walking in the Yang direction (10).

1

2

3

4

5

6

7

8

9

10

Snake

First Form: Snake Slithers Through the Grass

Walking form: Walk in the Yin direction on the circle, your head and eyes facing the middle. Your left arm is extended out toward the middle of the circle with your fingers pointing out at chin height. The left elbow is bent about thirty degrees and the palm is flat, with the fingers pointing to the center of the circle. The right palm is outside the right hip and pushing down, with the fingers pointing toward the right hip. Your eyes look out to the left palm (1).

- Right Ko Bu He Zhang. Keep your body, head, and eyes facing in the Yin direction. Bring your left palm in front of your chest near your right shoulder, just like the single palm change. Your right palm comes up underneath your left elbow, again like the single palm change (2).

- Left Bai Bu. Turn your body, head, and eyes in the Yang direction, keeping your arm posture. Again, this is just like the single palm change (3).

- Right over Ko Bu with right Tiao Zhang. Your head, eyes, and body all turn to face in the Yin direction. Your left hand pushes around to your right side, protecting your right ribs under your right armpit. At the same time, your right hand rises up as high as it can go, with the fingers pointing up. Extend and twist the arm and hand as much as you can, with your upper arm right next to your right ear. Your eyes are looking back over your left shoulder, creating a lot of twisting in the body. Your legs and body are sinking down (4).

- Left Pu Tui You Shen and Liao Zhang. Your body turns left as you extend your left leg back and bend the right knee. Your weight is on the right leg, almost sitting down. Your right palm pushes back with your fingers pointing down, arm fully extended. Your left shoulder, arm, and palm are twisting and extending. Move your hand behind the left hip, with palm facing up and your fingers twisting and following the line of the leg. From there, your body weight shifts from your right leg to your left leg into left Gung Bu. At the same time, the right palm keeps pushing back with the fingers down. The left shoulder, arm, and palm keep twisting, extending, and moving forward, ending at shoulder height. Your eyes look forward to your left palm. From there, your left palm moves up in Liao Zhang, with the pinkie on the top. Your arm keeps twisting and extending. This is called Pu Tui You Shen (5).

- Right Xu Bu. Your body keeps facing in the Yang direction. Your right palm is under your left armpit, and the left arm stays extended with the pinkie on top (6).

- Left Shi Bu. As you step forward with your right foot, extend your right arm out so the right hand moves underneath your left arm. The left hand withdraws to underneath the right armpit. The left foot comes up from behind into a left Shi Bu stance. Keep looking in the Yang direction (7).

- Right Shi Bu. Repeat the arm motion with the opposite hand. Everything else is the same (8).

- Left Shi Bu. Repeat the movement of number six (9).

- Your left foot moves back, then your right foot follows into a right Shi Bu, with your body sinking down very much. Both hands are brought back to just in front of your chin, with both palms up (10).

- Your right foot moves forward into a right half follow step. At the same time, the right palm extends to the center of the circle, and the left palm moves out and down to outside of the left hip. This is the walking form. Your eyes look out past the right palm (11).

- Begin walking in the Yang direction.

1

2

3

4

5

6

7

8

9

10

11

Second Form: White Snake Spits Out Tongue

Walking form: Walk in the Yin direction on the circle, with your eyes and head facing the center of the circle and your left arm pointed to the center of the circle, and with the palm up at chin height and the fingers strongly extended. The right arm is raised above your head, with the palm facing up above the Bai Hui point and the fingers pointing to the center of the circle (1).

- Right Ko Bu. Turn your head and eyes in the Yang direction on the circle. Turn your left palm over so it faces down and out, and move the arm so it points in the Yang direction of the circle. The fingers extend strongly. Turn your right palm over so it faces the center of the circle, bring it in front of your right shoulder, and strongly bend your right elbow. The elbow extends strongly in the Yin direction. The fingers of the right palm should strongly extend in the Yang direction of the circle (2).

- Left Bai Bu. Keep your head and eyes facing in the Yang direction and turn your body to face in the Yang direction. Your upper body and arms maintain their position (3).

- Left Gen Bu with right Truin Zhang. Keep your head, eyes, and body facing in the Yang direction. Step forward with your left foot into a left Gen Bu. As you do this, bring your left hand down to near your right ribs with the palm facing down. Then step forward with your right foot as you extend your right fingers straight out in the Yang direction, at chin height. This is the pattern of block and strike forward with the fingers, or Truin Zhang (4).

- Right Gen Bu with left Truin Zhang. Repeat the movement, still going in the Yang direction, using the opposite sides of your body (5).

- Left Gen Bu with right Truin Zhang. Repeat movement three, still going in the Yang direction (6).

- Right Ko Bu to left Tsuo Bu. Your back is directed to the center of the circle. Look in the Yang direction on the circle while standing on your left leg. Both palms come up to the chin, then the right palm, with the palm up and fingers first, leads in the Yang direction of the circle. At the same time, the left palm, with palm up and fingers first, leads in the Yin direction (7).

- Twist your body to the left, or counter clockwise, pivoting on the right leg. At the same time, the right palm goes overhead, then drops down in front of your face and chest, to block your chest. The palm is facing out, with the fingers sideways, pointing to the center of the circle. You are facing in the Yang direction and your palm is facing in the Yang direction. Then you continue to drop the palm and move it in front of the left ribs, again in the Truin Zhang position. As the right palm drops, extend the left palm out in the Yang direction, with the palm up and the fingers leading. At the same time, draw back the left foot into left Xu Bu. Then the left foot moves forward into a half left Gen Bu with the left Truin Zhang (8).

- Five-step circle. Step toward the center of the circle with your right leg (9).

- Continue to step, each time turning around ninety degrees, until you step back onto the larger circle on the fifth step (10).

- You should have now done a complete circle and should be facing in the Yang direction with your eyes facing the middle of the circle. As you start to step with your right foot, your left palm turns over to face down, and your right palm turns over to face up. Then the palms cross in front of the chest, and the right palm follows the body, making a circle. The left palm moves up from your left side and goes up over your head. As you make the five steps, your eyes follow the right palm. As you finish the fifth step, you should be in the walking position but facing in the Yang direction. Your eyes are looking to the center of the circle and your body is facing in the Yang direction. Both palms and arms extend strongly to the center of the circle (11).

- Begin to walk in the Yang direction. As you walk, you can draw back your arms just a bit until, at the finish of the five steps, they are seventy percent extended instead of one hundred percent.

1

2

3

4

5

6

7

8

9

10

11

Third Form: Double-Headed Snake

Walking form: The walking form is the same as the second form, except that the right palm pushes down from above. The right middle finger points to the Lao Gung point on the left palm (1).

- Right Ko Bu. Turn your head and eyes to face in the Yang direction, while you keep your body facing in the Yin direction. At the same time, swing your left arm horizontally until your fingers face in the Yang direction, with the left palm facing out and down and the arm and fingers strongly extended. The right palm drops down in front of the groin, with the palm pressing strongly down and the fingers pointed in the Yang direction (2).

- Left Bai Bu. Your eyes and head keep facing in the Yang direction, while your body turns to also face in the Yang direction. Your arms and palms keep their position (3).

- Right Gung Bu with right Truin Zhang. Keep facing in the Yang direction and take a big step into right Gung Bu as you strike out with your right palm in Truin Zhang (4).

- Your body turns into left Xu Bu. Turn your body counterclockwise 180 degrees to face in the Yin direction. As you do this, step into a left Xu Bu. Your right hand goes overhead, with the palm facing in the Yin direction and the fingers pointing inside the circle. The left palm goes down to near the left hip, with the fingers stretching down and the left palm facing in the Yang direction (5).

- Left Pu Tui You Shen Liao Zhang. This is the same as the basic Pu Tui You Shen Liao Zhang (6).

- Your body moves back into right reverse Gung Bu. Then you move back into left Gong Bu. As you move back into left Gong Bu, your right palm goes overhead and then in front of your face and chest. Then execute a left Truin Zhang, with the left hand striking out in the Yang direction (7).

- Then, turn your body to a regular right Gung Bu with a right Truin Zhang to the Yin direction (8).

- Again, turn into a left Gung Bu with a left Truin Zhang in the Yang direction (9).

- Your eyes and head follow the motion of the body.

- Right over Ko Bu. Look in the Yang direction, with your body facing the outside of the circle. Both arms cross in front of your body, with the right arm outside the left arm, the palms facing your body, and the fingers extending down (10).

- Shuang Chie Zhang. Continue to turn your body until you are facing the center of the circle. Step with your left foot into a big Ma Bu. At the same time, both palms chop down to protect the outsides of both legs. The palms face the legs, and the fingers extend down and out (11).

- Your body turns in the Yang direction into left Gung Bu, and then does a left Truin Zhang. Your eyes follow the left palm (12).

- Five-step circle. This is the same as the second snake form, except that you finish with the left palm facing down instead of up (13, 14, 15).

1

2

3

4

5

6

7

8

9

10

11

12

13

14

15

Dragon

First Form: Dragon Flying in the Clouds with Pian Zhang

Walking form: Walk in the Yin direction, with eyes and head facing the center of the circle. The body is twisting toward the center of the circle. Both palms are extended down in front of the left hip, with the fingers down and the palms facing the center of the circle. The edges of the palms are touching (1).

- Right Ko Bu. Your body continues to twist toward the center of the circle. Your head and eyes face the center of the circle. Turn your palms over and cross your forearms, with the right arm over the left. The palms should be facing your waist, with the fingers extended together (2).

- Left Bai Bu. Turn your body, head, and eyes to face in the Yang direction. Lift your arms overhead until the fingers are pointed upwards and the palms are facing in the Yang direction, with the forearms still crossed. Bring the palms out to the sides, palms up and fingers out. Then bring the edges of the palms together at chin height, with the arms extended and the fingers extending in the Yang direction. This is Shuang Pian Zhang, or double chopping in strike (3).

- Right over Ko Bu. Turn your body to face outside the circle, with your eyes looking in the Yang direction over your right shoulder. At the same time, drop down your arms in front of your body and cross them, similar to the first Ko Bu, again with the right arm over the left (4).

- Left Tsuo Bu. Turn your body to face in the Yin direction on the circle, with your eyes and head looking to the Yin direction. At the same time, both palms start to lift up (5).

- Right withdrawing step. Your body faces the center of the circle, and your head and eyes face in the Yang direction. Lift your hands up over your head, uncrossed, with the palms facing the center of the circle and the fingers strongly extended upward. The two hands just touch (6).

- Left Shun Bu into Ma Bu. Your body continues to face the center of the circle and your head and eyes continue to face in the Yang direction. Extend your hands out to the sides in a chopping down motion and then bring them to shoulder height, with the palms facing the center of the circle and the fingers extending out to either side (7).

- Right toe kick. Your right foot kicks forward with the toe. Both palms move down and in front of the outside of your right hip. Your upper body turns in to the center of the circle, and your head and eyes face the center of the circle. Your left leg is straight, as you stand up tall. Then bend the left leg to sink down the whole body, strongly extending both palms straight down. Bend your knees as much as you can, but do it slowly. Dropping slowly is actually harder and more beneficial, and is safer as well. As you practice slowly and carefully, you will find it easier to sink down more. Draw back your right foot and bend the knees. This is Ti Xi, or lift up knee (8).

- Then step with your right foot and begin walking in the Yang direction on the circle.

1

2

3

4

5

6

7   8

Second Form: Dragon Dives into the Ocean

Walking form: Walk and look in the Yin direction on the circle, with your palms out in front of your belly button, the palms up and touching, and the fingers extending in the Yin direction. Your elbows and forearms are together. Your elbows should be close to your body (1).

- Right Ko Bu. Continue to face in the Yin direction with your eyes, head, and body. Turn your palms over and cross them in front of your chest, with the right palm over the left palm. Your arms and hands stay extended out at belly button height (2).

- Double Pian Zhang, in two parts:

  1. Right step back with your left foot, but keep looking in the Yin direction. Then sink back on your left leg while still facing the Yin direction. Lift both hands above your head and uncross them, so the palms are facing in the Yin direction and the fingers are strongly pointed upward. Bring the palms out to either side of your body, with the palms up and the fingers extended. Then bring together the outside edges of both palms in front of your body at chin height, with the arms extended, the palms up, and the fingers extended. As you chop, shift your weight onto the right leg while moving your body slightly in the Yin direction (3).

2. Left Bai Bu. Pick up your left foot and turn into left Bai Bu. Your body turns to face in the Yang direction. Your head and eyes turn to face in the Yang direction. Both palms withdraw to both sides of the Dai Mai or waist. The palms are up and the fingers point to the Dai Mai. Your elbows are back and down, and you are sinking strongly on the right leg as you turn (4).

- Right over Ko Bu. Your head and eyes face in the Yang direction, looking over your right shoulder. Your body faces outside the circle. Keep pulling your palms back until you can point your fingers at your Ming Men points, with your fingers pointing in the Yang direction and the palms up. The elbows are drawn strongly behind you (5).

- Left Tsuo Bu. Your head and eyes turn to face in the Yin direction. Your body faces the inside of the circle. Both arms extend strongly out to the side and then swing in front of the body with the palms up at chest height. The sides of the palms are touching together (6).

- Right follow squeeze step. Your head and eyes turn to face in the Yang direction. Then your body turns to face in the Yang direction as well. Maintain your hand position as you turn (7).

- Left Shun Bu. Your eyes, head, and body keep facing in the Yang direction. Maintain your hand position as you turn (8).

- Right Xu Bu. Your eyes, head, and body keep facing in the Yang direction. Bend your left knee and sink down on the left leg. At the same time turn both palms to face down, drop your palms to groin height, and then turn the palms up and lift them up to the waist, about fifty percent extended.

- Right half follow step. Continue to face and look in the Yang direction. Strongly step forward with your right foot as you spear forward and down with the fingers of both palms. At the same time, strongly sink down on both feet as you finish the follow step. This is called Dun Bu Xia Cha Zhang, or sinking step double spearing down palm (9).

- Then, allow your hands to rise slightly to the level of the walk, as you begin to walk around the circle.

1

2

3

4

5

6

7

8

9

Third Form: Dragon Twirls in the Sky

Walking form: Walk in the Yin direction on the circle, with eyes and head looking to the center of the circle. The palms are extended to either side, with the palms up and the fingers pointing in the Yin and Yang directions, respectively. The arms are strongly extended out to the fingers at shoulder height (1).

- Right Ko Bu. Your body faces the center of the circle. Your eyes and head keep looking to the center. Extend your right hand down in front of your groin, with your hand in a "dragon claw" grip, with the fingers partly curled and strongly separated so they look like a big claw. Extend your left hand up above your head, also in a "dragon claw." Both of the palms face the center of the circle (2).

- Left Gung Bu. Turn your body to face in the Yang direction. Your eyes keep facing the center of the circle. Extend your right hand to the center of the circle at shoulder height, with the fingers pointed sideways and toward the center of the circle. The left hand maintains its position above your head, with the fingers pointed sideways and to the center of the circle (3).

- Right over Ko Bu. Turn your body to face outside the circle. Your eyes and head face in the Yang direction of the circle, looking over your right shoulder. Bring both hands above your head, still in dragon claw posture, with the hands a little bit apart and the claws pointing up. Your elbows are pointed to either side (4).

- Left Tsuo Bu. Turn your body to face the inside of the circle. Your eyes and head face in the Yin direction on the circle. Maintain your arm posture as you turn (5).

- Right follow-squeeze step. Turn your body, head, and eyes to face in the Yang direction on the circle. Maintain your arm posture as you turn (6).

- Left Shun Bu. Keep facing in the Yang direction and maintain your arm posture as you turn (7).

- Right foot steps forward. Keep your body facing in the Yang direction and look to the Yang direction. At the same time, both hands "claw" downward to either side, then inward toward the legs, then continue to make big circles in front of you. Both arms complete a full circle, so the palms end up at either side of your body at shoulder height (8). Then turn your palms over and extend the fingers into the walking form.

- Five-step inside circle (not shown). Start by looking to the center of the circle. Then take five small steps, starting with your right foot, to make an inside circle, maintaining the arm posture. When you finish, your eyes and head should be facing the center of the circle, your body should be facing the inside of the circle, and your arms are extended out to the Yin and Yang directions of the circle. Finish by strongly sinking down into your stance while you extend your fingers outward in a short and sharp motion. Then begin to walk in the Yang direction on the circle.

1

2

3

4

5

6

7

8

Eight Animals, Three Levels, and Their Connection to the *I Ching*

The organization of the movement patterns in these more intricate forms contain traditional concepts that can help you better understand, practice, and explore Bagua Zhang and its relationship to the *I Ching.* There are at least three big points to understand.

The *I Ching* is divided into three levels: earth, man, and heaven or sky. They are closely related. Man is in the middle because we are the "owners" of the universe, but it is also important that we should give respect to sky and earth, to nature. There should be wonderful harmony between the three levels. Bringing about this harmony is the number one job for human beings. The Twenty-Four Movements of Eight Animals form is focused on this idea of the three levels. The twenty-four movements are broken up into three different movements, expressing the three different levels: upper, middle, and lower; or earth, humanity, and the universe. When you practice this form, you should be feeling that you are a human being, trying to make wonderful harmony with everything.

At the same time, the whole form is based on the philosophy of the eight trigrams or Bagua map, as well as the philosophy of the five elements. For example, this form starts from the earth, with the Kun Gua. Then it changes into lion, which is sky, or Chian Gua. Then into bear, or mountain, with gun gua. Then into phoenix, or wind, with Xun Gua. Then into rooster, or fire, on the Li Gua. Then into monkey, or lake, with Dui Gua. Then into snake, or water, with Kan Gua. The last one is dragon, or thunder, with Zhen Gua. All of them, from earth to thunder, make a picture of the whole universe. And these fundamental forces of nature, or the eight trigrams, develop through the interaction of the five elements.

When you practice this form, you should use your body language to express a "beautiful picture" of the variety of forces in the universe in great harmony. The essence of the eight animal movements comes from the individual Bagua trigrams, and so this form makes the different movements that are basic to the nature of the different parts of the natural world and the universe. It can be a guide to connect to the natural world. It also can tell you how nice and beautiful it can feel when there is a good balance between the different parts of the universe. The different parts have strong influence on each other.

Human beings should pay attention to that; don't let one part hurt another part. Keep the whole universe balanced and beautiful. Again, this is the main job for human beings.

Finally, in traditional Chinese culture, it is thought that there were two other books that were much older than the *I Ching*. The first one is called *Lian Shan*. This book was made in the Xia Dynasty (from the twenty-first to the sixteenth century B.C.). The second book, called *Gui Cang,* was made during the Shang Dynasty (from the sixteenth century B.C. to 1027 B.C.). The *I Ching* is the third one, made during the Zhou Dynasty (from 1027 B.C. to 256 B.C.).

In the *Lian Shan,* the first trigram was the Gun Gua, or mountain. In the *Gui Cang,* the first trigram was the Kun Gua, or earth—the most Yin or feminine of the trigrams. At the time the *Gui Cang* was written, the woman was the ruler of the family; it was a matriarchal society. That is why the Kun Gua was the first of the eight trigrams: they respected the feminine. The first trigram of the *I Ching* is the Chian Gua, or heaven. The twenty-four movements of the eight animals starts on the Kun Gua as well. When Liu Bin and his Bagua brothers studied the Bagua Zhang and developed new forms, they researched and took ideas from the *Gui Cang.*

Martial Applications of Animal Forms

Although each of the animal forms can have many martial applications, we have explained one usage for each that is representative of that particular form. Once you know the movement well, it is fairly easy to use these in applications.

Chilin

First form: Chilin Pushes Down to the Earth. For the first chilin form, the essence of the martial application is within the first movement, Chilin Ta Di or Chilin Pushes Down to Earth. For example, if someone controls both of your wrists, the best way to protect yourself is to sink down strongly with your body and then separate the palms with a twisting motion. Turn the palms over with the fingers pointed in and then lift the palms quickly. This will remove the person's grip. Then, drop both palms very quickly as you step between the person's legs. This controls the opponent's centerline, and can be used to attack his chest, abdominal region, or groin.

Second form: Chilin Shoulders Mountain. This can be used when someone tries to punch or grab your chest. The scissoring motion as you cross your arms will block and trap the attacker, and you can turn your body to break his limb or throw him. If the opponent attacks with his right arm, you turn right. This moves you to his outside, where he cannot attack you. Then you push out with both palms on his chest or shoulder.

Third form: Chilin Pushes Up to the Sky. This can be used if a big person confronts you. When he comes to you, grab under his arm with both hands and push up to unbalance him, then twist your body to throw or injure him.

Lion

First form: Lion Holds the Ball. This one can be used in two main ways. If someone attacks you, you turn your body, sink down, and grasp his arm with your arms. Then, as you keep turning, you can throw or injure him. Again, if he uses his right arm, you should turn to the right side, locking the elbow and shoulder. The second way this can be used is if someone kicks at you. You move outside, sink down, and control the leg with one hand on the ankle and another on the knee. Then you can keep twisting to throw or injure your opponent.

Second form: Lion Grasps the Ball. In case someone grabs you with both hands, you circle the attacker's arms and grab him with yours, then drive in and claw at his abdomen or groin with a quick Gen Bu and Dun Bu.

Third form: Lion Rolling. If someone attacks you, use vertical circling to deflect, grab, and control his arm. If he attacks your upper body, start with the third step, when the hands are rising up. If he begins by attacking your lower body, start with the first step, when the hands are dropping. Once you control him, use the circling motion to throw or injure him.

Bear

First form: Bear Looking Back. When two people attack you from the front and the back, and each one controls one of your wrists, you extend both arms strongly and keep extending and twisting to throw them off. If that doesn't completely get rid of them, it will at least unbalance them. Then, if need be, you can change and use the palm motion to strike them, either in the head or groin.

Second form: Bear Holds Up Sun and Moon. When two people come to you, you need to move between them. Then you use the up/down striking motion to attack both of them at once. If two people control your wrists, you go between them and do the same movement. This will get rid of their control as you hit them. Again, if it doesn't work perfectly the first time, you can finish them off by changing and repeating the attack to the other side of the body, using the other arm.

Third form. Bear Pierces Earth and Sky. When two people control both your wrists, quickly move between them and spear up and down. This will release their grip as well as enable you to attack both people. Again, if it doesn't work, continue to move forward and strike by reversing the movement.

Phoenix

First form: Phoenix Folds Wings Back. You can quickly move to the side of a person and "wash his face" with a Ma Mien Zhang. One arm catches his arm while you step behind him and strike with the other arm. If two people are attacking at the same time, you should get between them and attack both at the same time, one to the face, the other to the groin.

Second form: Phoenix Starts to Open Wings. You move to the side of the person's body and use the double chop down to the shoulder blades, the clavicle, or other points on the shoulders.

Third form: Phoenix Flying. If a person controls one or both of your wrists, you use the movement of dropping the palms down and turning them over to break the control and grab the arm. You can turn to throw him or, if you prefer, you can spear him.

Rooster

First form: Rooster Bends Wings. If someone kicks at you from behind, you use the number two movement, Sa Zhang or opening the net. This will block the kick. Then use the Gai Zhang or dropping palm. You can control the kicker's ankle with the outside of the thumb and wrist, making the palm strike much more effective. If a person controls your wrist, you can move forward toward him, and use moves seven and eight to unbalance, strike, and throw him.

Second form: Golden Rooster Crows in the Morning. If someone comes at you, you use moves six through eight to block-punch in a continuous fashion to overwhelm him. If someone controls your wrist, use the last movement to clear the arm away and break the wrist.

Third form: Rooster Eating Rice. When the person controls your wrist, you move toward him face to face. At the same time, take your wrist back to your collarbone. At the same time, drive the back of your wrist into his chin and neck. If the person manages to block your wrist, change to movement six or seven, go around his block, and use the rooster fingers to strike the temple, eyes, or another target.

Monkey

First form: Monkey Holds Cauldron. This movement has two functions. If you do it slowly, the exercise is good for developing internal chi. If you do it quickly and powerfully, the application is called Bao Zhang or holding palm. When you are very close to someone, you can attack with Bao Zhang.

Second form: Five Flower Hand. This application is called Five Flower Palm or Wu Hao Sho and can be used in case someone grabs your wrist. Use the twisting movement to remove his grip, then use the Zhuang Zhang (hard punch with palm) to attack him.

Third form: Monkey Offers Fruit. In case someone is attacking or grabbing at your chest or head, use the back of the palm with Fan Zhang (turning palm) to block. Then use the Truin Zhang motion to spear at his eyes or throat.

Snake

First form: Snake Slithers Through the Grass. Using movement three, you turn and attack with the shoulder. The rising arm helps to uproot the opponent and then the shoulder hits him. Continue to use Truin Zhang, movements four through six, against someone who is behind you.

Second form: White Snake Spits Out Tongue. This one is used to protect your back and to fight back with Truin Zhang, movements one through five.

Third form: Double-Headed Snake. The function of this form is continuous attacking using Truin Zhang. All three of these forms emphasize the different ways you can use Truin Zhang, and the applications will become clear once you have a good foundation of practice.

Dragon

First form: Dragon Flying in Clouds with Pian Zhang. In case the enemy attacks your lower body or groin, you protect with Jiao Cha Zhang or crossing over palms. Then you use Shuang Pian Zhang, double strike with the edge of your palm, to fight back.

Second form: Dragon Dives into the Ocean. In case someone attacks your chest or lower body, use the An Zhang motion or movement one to block. Then use Shuang Pian Zhang followed by a Shuang Cha Zhang, or double downward strike.

Third form: Dragon Twirls in the Sky. In case someone controls your wrists, you use the opening arm motion, Jiao Cha Zhang, and continue to walk the circle to remove the grip and unbalance him.

GLOSSARY

Ai Beng Ji Kao—get close to your opponent and use your whole body

Ba Xiong Di—literally, brothers from different families; a term for close lifelong friends

Ban Li—being better conditioned; training for strength and endurance

Bagua Guan Dao—Bagua big curved sword

Bagua Jia Jiao Ge Ge Bai Rao—by using Bagua skills and wrestling techniques, you can defeat anybody

Bagua Jian—Bagua big straight sword

Bai Bu—opening step, in which the toes separate as you step

Bai Hui—point on top of the head

Bai Kou Huan Bu—an advanced variation on the single palm change, in which you start the change with your inside foot

Bao Tui—"holding the leg" technique of Chinese wrestling

Bei Shen Zhang—bear palm, third of the eight mother palms; an advanced form of Pu Tui You Shen

Bai Yu Cai—best student of Wang Wen Kui

Bao San—famous Chinese wrestler

Beng—wood, one of Hsing-I's five "fists"

Bi Cheng Xia—Taoist master, teacher of Dong Hai Chuan

Bian Zhi Zhon—Taoist teacher, known for teaching Taoist longevity chi gong practices; one of the author's chi gong teachers

Bie Tze—controlling the opponent's legs with your own legs to throw him

Bing Bu—one-footed stance

Bu—step or stance; generally understood in Chinese martial arts as stance, but in Bagua it refers to the stepping action that ends in a stance

Bu Ding Bu Ba Zhi Bu—small Ko Bu step

Chang Bao Zhang—famous Chinese martial artist

Change—a direction change while walking the Bagua circle or, in a more general sense, any sort of change

Channels—the "rivers of energy" that flow through the body, out to the limbs, and back into the internal organs; also known as acupuncture meridians or meridians

Chen Jian Chui Chou—both shoulders and elbows dropping down, along with hands

Cheng Pai Liu Shi Bagua—another name for Liu Bin's Bagua; literally, it means Cheng style, Liu school Bagua

Cheng Ting Hua—one of the top students of Dong Hai Chuan, and teacher of numerous Bagua masters, including Liu Bin

Chi—the internal energy developed through Bagua or other chi gong practices; chi can also mean any kind of energy, like heat, light, wind, or electricity

Chi Bu—Horse Stance; fifty-fifty stance

Chi gong—training to develop internal energy or chi

Chi sphere—the area in and around your body where chi circulates

Chi Xing Bu—seven stars stepping; the principle stepping pattern of the twenty-four animals forms

Chian Gua—the northwest corner of the Bagua map, associated with the lion

Chiao—ingenious

Ching Dynasty—also known as the Manchu dynasty, it was the last ruling dynasty of China, from 1644 to 1912

Ching Gong—lightness skill; the skill of super jumping or near flying

Chilin—mythical Chinese animal, similar in some ways to a unicorn

Chong Wen Men—the gate of Chong Wen, a famous place in Beijing

Choung—extending and pressing out

Choung Guo Li—extending and withdrawing at the same time; an important concept in developing internal strength

Chu Xi—letting the knees bend to sink into your stance

Chuai—to kick backward with the entire sole of the foot

Chuang Tse—Taoist master, credited with writing one of the most important Taoist texts

Chuan Fang Wei—movement that is spiraling, smooth, and changeable

Circle walk—walking in a circle, the main practice of Bagua Zhang

Cui Yu Ke—student of Liu Xing Han and member of Liu's book writing group

Chuo—big toe pointed down to ground

Confucius—Chinese philosopher and scholar; the founder of Confucianism

Cuan Beng Tiao Yue—jumping higher and/or farther

Cultural Revolution—a time of great political upheaval in China, from 1966 to 1976

Da Chou Tian Gong—large heavenly circle

Dai Mai—the belt meridian; circles the waist at a level just below the umbilicus

Dan Bai Dan Ko—single turning change step

Ding Shi—special Bagua standing meditation, which develops the twisting of the hips and legs

Dong—to kick forward with the entire sole of the foot

Dong Jing Je He—combining of the internal and external

Dong Hai Chuan—the originator of modern Bagua Zhang and teacher of Cheng Ting Hua

Du Channel—a meridian that runs up the back, from the perineum to the top of the head, and down the face; this channel governs all the Yang channels of the body

Dui Gua—the west side of the Bagua map, associated with the monkey

Dun—body sinking down, bent knees

Fa Jin—expressing power; a sharp, small, fast movement designed to generate and use internal power

Five Elements—earth, metal, water, wood, fire; the theory of how the energy and matter of the body and world interact

Fu—the solid organs of the body; part of the Zhang/Fu theory of traditional Chinese medicine

Gen Bu—follow step; after stepping forward, bring your back foot in close behind the front foot

Gen Gua—the northeast corner of the Bagua map, associated with the bear

Gong—bow stance

Gou Gua Bu—hooking foot step; a variation on the Ko Bu step

Gu Yan Chu Chun—single goose leaves the flock; refers to a movement within single palm change

Gua—one of the eight sections of the Bagua map; for example, if you are walking the circle and you change direction at the northernmost part of the circle, you could say that you changed on the Kan Gua

Gun Zhe Jing—twisting the body to move close to your opponent

Guo—withdrawing in

Guo Ko Bu—over Ko Bu step; like a Ko Bu, but your front foot goes farther, past the back toes

Guo Xue Xin—student under Wang Rong Tang and member of Liu's book writing group

Guo Yun Shen—Hsing-I master and student of Dong Hai Chuan

Guo Feng De—third-generation Bagua master; part of the Nan Cheng Wu Lao

Han—Chinese ethnic group, vastly larger than any other group

Han De—grandson of Han Wu, seventh-generation Bagua master

Han Wen—fifth generation Cheng Bagua master

Han Wu—brother of Han Wen; fifth-generation Bagua master; studied with both Master Chang Guo Xing and Master Liu Shi Kui

He Pu Ren—a very famous Chinese doctor who studied under fourth-generation master Wang Dian Rong; vice president of the Chinese acupuncture association and member of Liu Xing Han's book writing group

He Xin—student of Liu Xing Han and member of Liu's book writing group

Heaven Temple Park—also called Tian Tan Park, a traditional practice place for Bagua Zhang

Heng—earth, one of Hsing-I's five "fists"

Heng Kai Zhang—literally horizontal opening palm; another name for the single palm change

Hsing-I—Chinese internal martial art, emphasizing Yang, or hard strength

Hua Shi—an area in southern Beijing where Cheng Ting Hua worked

Huai Bao Chi Xing—holding the seven stars; another name for the single palm arm posture

Huai Bao Dan Yu—holding single fish; another name for the single palm arm posture

Huai Bao Yin Yang—holding the Yin and Yang; another name for the single palm arm posture

Hui Yin—point at base of pelvis, in the perineum area

I-Ching—classic book of changes; the Chinese theory of how the mind can understand and work with the processes of change in the universe; also used as an oracle

Ji Feng Xiang—third-generation Bagua master; part of the Nan Cheng Wu Lao

Jianzi Tui—squeezing the thighs and knees together as you walk

Jiao Bie Tze—throwing, using primarily the legs

Jiu Hua Shan—Nine Flowers Mountain, in An Hui province

Jiu Jie Bian—nine-section metal weapon, used by Liu Bin

Kan Gua—the north side of the Bagua map, associated with the snake

Ko Bu—closing step, in which the toes come relatively closer together as you step

Ko Bu He Zhang—closing palm with closing step; the first move of the single palm change

Kun Gua—the southwest corner of the Bagua map, associated with the chilin

Kun Ming city—a city in Yunan province

Lao Tzu—literally, old man; Taoist master credited with writing the Tao Te Ching

Le Tai platform—a tall platform that was the equivalent of a boxing ring for Chinese martial arts matches

Li—heel pointed down to ground

Li Gua—the south side of the Bagua map, associated with the rooster

Li Guo Gun—student of Liu Xing Han from Henan province

Lian Hua—water lily palm

Liao Zhang—rising palm, used in Pu Tui You Shen and other movements

Lao Gung—point in the middle of the palm

Li He Ting—third-generation Bagua master; part of the Nan Cheng Wu Lao

Li Wen Zhang—student of Wang Rong Tang

Li Yan Chin—the top student of Liu Bin and fourth-generation Bagua master

Li Zhang—lifting up palms position; a movement within single palm change

Li Zhi Wai Kou—all of the leg mechanics of the Bagua walk

Li Zong Chuan—student of Liu Xing Han

Liu Bin—student of Cheng Ting Hua, third-generation Bagua master; also known as Kuin Chuan

Liu Chuang—son of Liu Xing Han and member of Liu's book writing group

Liu Feng Chun—youngest student of Dong Hai Chuan

Liu Jing Liang—student of Liu Xing Han; teaches in Yunan province and worked with Zhang Jie and Li Zong Chuan on the third Bagua book

Liu Mao Shing—student under Liu Xing Han and member of Liu's book writing group

Liu Shi Kui—student of Liu Bin

Liu Shui Bagua—Cheng Bagua, from Master Cheng You Long and Cheng You Xin, sons of Cheng Ting Hua

Liu Xing Han—leader of fourth generation, teacher of Zhang Jie

Lang Fang Tou Tiao—a business district in south Beijing

Lohan—Chinese martial arts style

Ma Gan Ji—literally, long whip Ji; another name for Ji Feng Xiang

Ma Gui Bao—student of Bao San and a famous Chinese wrestler

Ma Jian Xing—student of Liu Xing Han; president of the Beijing sport research institute and member of Liu Xing Han's book writing group

Ma Yin Tsang Xiang—advanced chi gong skill in which the practitioner can withdraw the male sex organs into his body at will; literally, withdraw your sex organs like a horse

Ma Yu Kuan—great painter and member of Liu's book writing group

Manchu—Chinese ethnic group, leaders of China during the Ching Dynasty

Me Ging—brushing your outside ankle with your inside ankle as you step

Mei Hui Chi—student under Wang Rong Tang and member of Liu's book writing group

Mei Lan Fang—a master of Chinese opera

Meridians—same as channels, part of the energetic anatomy of the body

Mian—bent knees and closed legs to protect the groin

Mian Ruan—soft and relaxed

Ming Dynasty—a ruling dynasty of China, from 1368 to 1644

Ming Men—two important points on the Dai Mai, near the kidneys on each side of the body

Nan Cheng Bagua—the common name for the Bagua of the south district of Beijing, where Liu Bin and other students of Cheng Ting Hua studied and taught

Nan Cheng Wu Lao—the five old masters of south district Bagua: Liu Bin, Li He Ting, Ji Feng Xiang, Liu Zhan Zong, and Guo Feng De

Nei Gong—inner work; more advanced chi gong practice

Nei Wai Jei He—combining of spirit, thoughts, chi, and movement

Pai Wei—a ceremony that is done to become an official student of a master

Palm—as in Bagua Zhang, "eight trigrams palm"; "palm" denotes both that it is a fighting art and that the open hand is emphasized in this style

Pan—bend knee deeply, almost like you are sitting cross-legged on the ground

Pao—fire, one of Hsing-I's five "fists"

Peng Lu Ji An—the four primary energies of Taiji Chuan

Pi—metal, one of Hsing-I's five "fists"

Ping Shan—the Bagua name of Liu Xing Han, given to him by Liu Bin

Points—acupuncture points located on the channels; also striking points, where you would strike someone

Pu—one leg extending, close to the ground

Pu Tui You Shen—turning back palm; a movement variation within single palm change

Ren Ai—connection between people through a feeling of love and compassion

Ren and Du channels—energy channels or meridians located on the midline of the torso, both back and front

Ren Channel—meridian that runs from the face to the perineum, down the front of the body; this channel governs all the Yin channels of the body

San Cai—man, heaven, and earth

San Huang Pao Chui—a martial arts style derived from Shaolin

Shen Bai Bu—turning body back with opening step

Si Zheng Si Yu—literally, four corners, four sides; an advanced palm form

Sha Hui Hui—martial arts master who worked for the Su Wang family as security

Shan Pu Ying—the training group of the Ching dynasty bodyguards

Shang Bu—forward step; taking a full step straight forward.

Shao Li—coordinated whole body movement

Shaolin—Chinese martial art style, originated in Shaolin Temple

Shi Liu Duan Jin—sixteen exercises of silk

Shi Ren Yi Rou, Shi Ren Yi Ruo—the principle of showing others your soft side

Rou Ruo Sheng Gang Chiang—the principle of soft overcoming hardness

Shing Mao Ting—student of Liu Xing Han and member of Liu's book writing group

Shou Bie Tze—throwing, using primarily the arms

Shou Yan Shenfa Bu—the principle of coordinating and connecting your hand, your body, your eyes, and your legs

Shu—to understand and forgive

Shuang Bai Shuang Ko—double turning change step

Shuang Ta Zhang—pressing down palms position, the basic circle walk arm posture

Shuai Jiao—Chinese wrestling

Shun Bu—natural step or correcting step; a short or half step that untwists the legs

Si Liu Bu—turning into a back stance; used in Zou Ma Huo Xi or running horse

Single palm—one of the main arm postures and changes in Bagua Zhang

Song Chang Rong—Bagua master who developed his own method of Bagua Zhang training

Su Wang—Beijing government officials who hired Dong Hai Chuan, first as a serving boy, later as head of their security force

Suo—sitting down, as in meditation

Suo Xiao—keeping your energy and chi inside, making a small movement

Ta—extending and pressing out

Ta Yao Liou Tung—letting the tailbone drop

Tai Ji—the center point, where Yin and Yang originate from and return to

Taiji Bagua Map—the map or symbol of the eight trigrams with the Yin-Yang symbol in the center; a traditional map of the inner laws of the world and universe

Taiji Chuan—Chinese martial art brought to Beijing by Yang Lu Chang

Tan Tien—energy center of the body, generally meaning the lower Dan Tian, located in the abdomen about one inch below the belly button in the center of the body

Tan Tong—area in Heaven Temple Park where Liu Bin and others traditionally practiced

Tan Xin Pei—master of Chinese opera and one of the founders of modern Chinese opera

Taoism—one of the main philosophical bases of Chinese culture as well as a mystical spiritual path

Ta—pressing down

Ti—lift up and bend knees

Ti En Fang—student of Liu Shi Kui; at the time of writing, he is the oldest living master of Zhuang Gong Bagua Zhang

Tiao Zhang—lifting up palm or hand

Tian Chao—a public area in southern Beijing and favorite place of Zhang Jie as a child

Tian Di—heaven and earth

Tian Ren He Yi—when a person becomes united with nature in a spiritual manner

Tie Dan Gong—making the middle of the groin strong as metal

Truin Zhang—block with one hand while striking with the other

Tsuan—water, one of Hsing-I's five "fists"

Tsuo Bu—an extended Bai Bu type of step, in which both feet are turned out, similar to the Ding Shi standing exercise

Tui Na—Chinese medical massage

Tuo Tian Zhang—lifting arms up to heaven, a movement of single palm change

Wai Mian Ruan, Nei Han Gang Bao Zhi Li—basically, the ability to make the body very soft or very hard at will, using the internal chi; literally soft like cotton, hard as metal

Wang Dan Ling—third-generation Bagua master; part of the Nan Cheng Wu Lao

Wang Rong Tang—a fourth-generation Bagua master who learned under Master Yang Ming Shan and member of Liu Xing Han's book writing group

Wang Wen Kui—student of Liu Bin, also known as "Uncle" Wang

Wang Zhen Ting—son of Wang Wen Kui

Wei—the protective energy of the body, as in Wei Chi

Wen Gu Er Zhi Xin—Confucian concept of always going back and working on the basics, of returning to study something more

Wu De—martial morality

Wu Chin Xi—five animals chi gong exercise

Wu Ji—literally, not something or emptiness

Wu Wei Wu Bu Wei—the principle of making the right choices about what to do and what not to do in order to create harmony

Wuo—one leg crossed behind the other leg, with the body sinking down

Xao Yao Bu Xing Gong—relaxed walking exercise

Xi Xiong Jen Bei—the back is curved and expanding, the front of the chest is open and curved slightly inward

Xia Pan—building a strong root and great balance

Xia Si Gong—to spend your time practicing, or someone who practices a lot over a lifetime

Xiao Hai Xue—student of Liu Xing Han from Guichou province

Xiao Zhou Tian Gong—small heavenly circle

Xie Fu De—student of Liu Xing Han from Shandong province

Xing—introspection, looking inside yourself to see your flaws clearly

Xing Ming Shuang Xiu—the combining of movement and quiet, related to the controlling of the mind or "monkey mind"

Xing Yun Cai—student of Liu Xing Han from Guangxi province

Xuan Ding—keeping the top of the head lifted up, one of the basic principles of Bagua practice

Xuan Ding Shu Xang—lifting the top of the head and keeping the chin in a neutral position, not stuck out; for many people, the neutral position feels like it is being pulled gently back

Xun Gua—the southeast corner of the Bagua map, associated with the phoenix

Yan Kou Huan Shi—changing direction while walking the circle or single palm

Yang—the principle of firmness or the masculine aspect

Yang Xiao Lou—a master of Chinese opera

Yang Zhang—litterally, lifting palms

Ye Di Cang Hua—flower hidden under the leaves; a traditional Chinese concept, it also refers to a movement within single palm change

Yi Jin Jing—change tendons and body to strengthen and relax at the same time

Yi Sheng Er, Er Sheng San, San Shang Wan Wu—Taoist philosophy of everything having originated from one source

Yin—the principle of softness or the feminine aspect

Ying—nutritional energy, coming from the food we eat

Yong Guang—the Bagua name of author Zhang Jie, given to him by Liu Xing Han; its meaning is to help Bagua develop so it can continue forever

You De Gen—student of Liu Xing Han from Hunan province

Zhan Zhuang Gong—standing and rooting meditation

Zhang organs—part of the categorizing of the internal organs according to traditional Chinese medicine; Zhang means the hollow organs

Zhang/Fu organs—the categorizing of internal organs into hollow (Zhang) and solid (Fu) categories, part of traditional Chinese medicine

Zhang Zhan Qui—Hsing-I master

Zhao Min Hua—student of Liu Xing Han and member of Liu's book writing group

Zhe—bent knees and leaving the foot behind the other knee

Zi Wu Yin Yang Yuan Yang Yue—special small double sword form; the Yue is like a dagger, but with additional edges built into the butt and handle

Zhen Gua—the east side of the Bagua map, associated with the dragon

Zhu—family name for the leading family during the Ming Dynasty

Zhu Zhen Hua—student of Liu Shi Kui

Zhuang Gong Bagua—part of Cheng Bagua, from Master Liu Bin and the Nan Cheng Wu Lao

Zou Ma Huo Xi—running horse, a movement variation within single palm change

Zou Yao—waist movement

Zuo Shen—keeping the head, neck, and shoulders relaxed and letting the shoulders sink; basic principle of Bagua practice